JOURNEYS
NOT REGRETTED

Edward Fischer and his wife, Mary, in South Bend, Indiana

JOURNEYS
NOT REGRETTED

The Columban Fathers'
Sixty-five Years in the Far East

Edward Fischer

Crossroad · New York

1986
The Crossroad Publishing Company
370 Lexington Avenue, New York, N.Y. 10017

Library of Congress Cataloging in Publication Data

Fischer, Edward.
Journeys not regretted.

1. Missions—East Asia. 2. St. Columban's Foreign
Mission Society. 3. Fischer, Edward. I. Title.
BV3400.F57 1986   266'.25   85-26986
ISBN 0-8245-0735-5

Contents

·1·

The Way It Started

On a convent wall in Tokyo hangs a poster: "The starting points of human destiny are little things." Important events in our lives often arrive by happy chance. A fortuitous happening, which some people call serendipity, Christian writers call providential.

Such an incident occurred Saturday morning, April 6, 1974. A phone call to my home brought an invitation for breakfast at the Morris Inn on the Notre Dame campus. A man I had never met wanted to tell me "about an archbishop in Korea."

My host at breakfast, a gentleman from Minneapolis, spoke of his friend Harold Henry who had been born in Minnesota, had spent his youth and middle years as a missionary in Korea, and was now an archbishop there.

After telling anecdotes about the archbishop for half an hour, my host asked, "Would that make a good book?"

"A very good book!" I said.

"Will you write it?"

"Yes," I said without hesitation and immediately began wondering why I had agreed. Why take leave from a Notre Dame classroom to face the rigors of research, travel and writing? Besides, I had never heard of Harold Henry and knew little about Korea.

To back out I said, "Maybe we won't get along."

"Archbishop Henry will be at the College of Saint Thomas next month for an honorary degree," said the man from Minneapolis. "He could come to Notre Dame at that time and the two of you could see if you get along."

Still trying to back out I asked my host why he had decided that I should tell the archbishop's story. He explained that his daughter had given him my book, *Why Americans Retire Abroad*, as a Christmas gift and that he had delayed reading it until on a spring holiday in Florida. All the while he was reading the book he kept saying to himself that the man who wrote this is the one who should write the archbishop's biography. And so on his way back to Minneapolis he had stopped at Notre Dame to make this request.

I said that I saw no relationship between retired Americans living abroad and an archbishop working in Korea. He admitted that neither could he, but that the idea just kept haunting him.

I had to admit that it also "felt right" to me. Long ago I learned that when something has the feeling of rightness about it you had better follow through. If you don't, everything starts going haywire.

When Archbishop Henry arrived at the South Bend airport it was evident, even before his baggage came down the chute, that we could get along together. He told anecdotes about life on the missions and I listened late into the night. The next morning I put him on a plane for his return to Korea.

That evening I took an Aer Lingus flight to Ireland. Since Harold Henry was a member of Saint Columban's Foreign Mission Society, the best place for me to make a start would be in the archives of the Society's world headquarters in Killiney, on the Irish Sea not far from Dublin.

Above the Atlantic that night I never dreamed that the assignment would go beyond one book. As it happened, after the biography, *Light in the Far East*, was published, a series of fortuitous happenings led me to write books about Harold Henry's confreres in Burma, China, Japan, Fiji and the Philippines.

During the next decade I explored Oriental cultures, exotic religions and the lives of missionaries. Because I took an early retirement I could give full time to the work. The routine was usually the same: First, go to the archives in Ireland and search for official reports, letters, diaries, magazine articles and newspaper stories. Then take this material to Notre Dame and begin absorbing it while using the university's library to research the country that, for the moment, was the focus of my attention. After a few months go to that country, live with missionaries and travel enough so that things learned in the archives would come alive. Then back to Notre Dame to write the story.

After each manuscript was finished several Columbans who had spent most of their lives in the country of which I was writing would give the pages a sentence-by-sentence, even a word-by-word reading. My main uneasiness was not about facts; if there was a wrong date or a wrong name the missionaries could readily correct that. My main concern was with the spirit reflected in the manuscript. Does it ring true? Is this how it felt to be a missionary at that time, in that place? Does it tell, as a good piece of writing must, how it is to be human under certain circumstances?

I realized that no amount of doctoring could save a manuscript if the missionaries found it false-spirited. That would have been the case where every fact is provable but the thing as a whole lacks the ring of authenticity. Fortunately, the veteran missionaries gave each manuscript a favorable review.

This memoir is begun on the tenth anniversary of my meeting with the man from Minneapolis. I want to recollect anecdotes that are already beginning to sound unreal and recall some unusual people I met in the Far East.

Fortunately, the satisfying experience of writing the series of books was delayed until my sixth decade of life. By then I was better prepared than ever to reach conclusions about remote countries, alien cultures and unfamiliar religions. The experiences changed some of my ways of looking at things, something unusual so late in life.

It was a good time, the years between my sixtieth and seventieth birthdays. Those were journeys not regretted.

·2·

A Most Colorful Fellow

Before meeting Archbishop Harold Henry I had become acquainted with only one other Columban, Father James Stuart. When I came to know him in Burma, in 1944, he had put aside his white soutane for the duration to participation in the Second World War. He dressed for the occasion: paratrooper boots, dark green combat fatigues with a piece of yellow parachute cloth knotted at the throat, all topped by an Aussie hat, the broad brim turned up rakishly at one side. He was a most colorful fellow.

While in India, waiting to cross the border into Burma, I heard stories about the Irish Columban from Derry. One of them had to do with the time an American intelligence officer complained of not having any Japanese prisoners of war to interview. He told Father Stuart, "Prisoners are so rare the British have a standing offer: two weeks' furlough to any Tommy who brings one in."

"I know where a Japanese is," said the priest, baiting the complaining American. "But he won't talk."

"He'll talk!" said the American. "You just take me to him."

The priest led the intelligence officer across three hills, mumbling all the way, "I know he won't talk. I know he won't." After working through some tall elephant grass and wading two mountain streams, they came to a remote bamboo basha.

"I told you he won't talk!" said Father Stuart pointing to a sleeping Japanese baby.

As one of eight Columban fathers from Ireland, James Stuart had arrived in Burma, late in 1936, to serve as a missionary to the Kachins in the northern wilderness. He never expected to see anything of war until, on May 13, 1942, a runner arrived at his remote parish bearing a message. It was from a British colonel saying that thousands of refugees were straggling into northern Burma just ahead of the Japanese. The colonel had hundreds on his hands. What to do?

Within an hour the missionary was hurrying by foot across the forty miles of jungle trail between Kajihtu and Sumprabum, where the British colonel asked him to accept forty-nine refugees. Twenty-five were children from a Church of England orphanage in Rangoon and the rest were women. They had walked a thousand miles with the vague notion that this route across mountains and through jungles would take them to India.

The refugees greeted the priest in near hysteria. Then suddenly, without warning, into the middle of all the confusion walked the Japanese.

Were it not for the refugees, Father Stuart would have fled with the Kachins and blended into the jungle. But now he had to stay and do some playacting.

So as not to be suspected of spying, he played the role of a simple fellow, hoping the Japanese would consider him harmless and lose interest. Father Stuart did the most naive thing he could think of: He walked out into the middle of the trail and stood there waiting for the Japanese major to approach on horseback.

"You Chinese?" Father Stuart asked.

The major spit and said, "Japanese!"

"You English?" asked the major.

The man from Derry spit and said, "Irish!"

The major dismounted, took a sword in one hand and a pistol in the other, and began a deliberate inspection of the missionary. Slowly he circled him, making hissing sounds as he sucked air through his teeth.

"Where Irish?" he asked.

The priest took the tall stick he carried, something of a shepherd's staff, and drew a circle in the clay.

"United States," he said.

Six feet away he drew another circle.

"England."

Not wanting Ireland to appear too near either the United States or England, he drew it in mid-Atlantic.

There on the trail the major held a long conference with his staff. After much sucking of air through teeth they decided they could not remember declaring war on any Ireland. And besides the simple soul seemed harmless. He had enough trouble with those hysterical women and screaming children. Let him go.

Later General Joseph Stilwell said: "The biggest mistake the Japanese made was not taking Father Stuart prisoner."

Father Stuart and his confrere, Father Denis McAlindon, both half-starved and filled with fever, worked themselves to exhaustion finding rice during the monsoon to keep the refugees alive. Then after five months they collected enough coolies and elephants to take the women and children from Sumprabum to Fort Hertz up near the Himalayas. From there they would be taken by air to India.

By now the missionaries looked so wraithlike that a British officer ordered them to India for rest and medical care. Hardly had their plane landed when they began pulling strings for a return trip to Burma. Absolutely not, said Major General Pearce, the chief of civil affairs in Burma. He added that since the missionaries had done so much for the government they were assured of food and housing in India for the duration.

Just when it looked as though the British general would have his way, the two priests were offered a return trip under the auspices of a hush-hush outfit, a group of Americans who called themselves Detachment 101. It was a unit of the Office of Strategic Services (OSS) dedicated to espionage and sabotage.

Father Stuart, accustomed to pulling other people's legs, thought that these bizarre Americans were pulling his. Especially when they told him that some of their instructors in the States had been selected from among the nation's top criminals. Who could better teach someone how to crack a safe, pick a pocket or forge a document than those who had spent their lives dedicated to developing such talents?

So that the OSS could put agents behind enemy lines, the Kachins built an airstrip of sorts—on a slant and somewhat curved. On it they placed portable huts. When a plane wanted to land the natives hurriedly carried off the huts, like stage scenery, and replaced them after the plane had departed.

The commanding officer of Detachment 101 saw right off that Father Stuart was his kind of fellow. Besides, the Kachins who knew the wilderness and every trail in it respected the priest and would do anything he asked.

One of the OSS assignments, the commanding officer explained to the missionary, was to rescue American airmen. They frequently crashed onto the Hump, on the India-China flight across the Himalayas. Would the missionary and his Kachins help save lives?

Soon after this meeting, Father Stuart found an American fighter pilot tangled on a tree limb sixty feet up in the air. The priest yelled, "Drop your parachute!" When the chute hit the ground he unzipped the pocket containing emergency rations and calmly sat beneath the tree, enjoying a rare treat—real chocolate.

Up among the branches the American began fuming and shouting.

"Be patient, lad, be patient," admonished the priest. "The Kachins will be along to get you down. Unless the Japanese hear you complaining."

Then it dawned on the pilot: "Are you Father Stuart?"

"Who else would be stupid enough to be in this part of the world?"

On another occasion a pilot mistaking a Kachin for a Japanese ran to the Irrawaddy, swam it and hid in a bamboo thicket. Moments later the bamboo parted and there stood the Kachin. He handed the exhausted pilot a note that had been scribbled by Father Stuart: "I am a friend. Follow me."

Refugees once more became the missionary's burden. He was asked to lead 241 of them—mostly women, children and old men—on a twenty-one-day trek in January of 1944. Rain fell almost incessantly, starvation was ever present and the Japanese were near.

Father Stuart described the events of one day, January 29: "It was a hard journey and about five miles of it meant wading upstream in a knee-deep river. It was very difficult for the children and for the blind women. There were heavy thunderstorms and everybody felt very cold being wet through and through. We came upon a village that had been abandoned for a year and wild elephants had knocked down all the houses. We put up some temporary shelters. No rice was available. Our patrols went out to search for game, or even buffalo left behind by the villagers, but had no success. Some of the refugees were sick and some had developed sore feet and swollen joints."

Those refugees, though, were fortunate that Father Stuart was in charge. Thousands of others did not do nearly so well. As Dr. Gordon Seagrave, the Burma surgeon, wrote: "There were skeletons around every water hole, lying sprawled out where the refugees had collapsed. At the front of every ascent were the bones of those who had died rather than attempt one more climb, and all up the hills were the bones of those who had died trying. Still standing along the road were some extremely crude shacks, each with its ten or twenty skeletons of those who couldn't get up when a new day came. In one of the shallow streams we were horrified to find that the Chinese had placed a long row of skulls to be used as stepping stones."

Father Stuart felt a sense of relief at Naw Bum where he and his refugees met up with an American unit called Merrill's Marauders. These volunteer infantrymen had the job of pushing the Japanese back yard by yard so that the engineers might build the Ledo Road over mountains and through jungles, from India across Burma to China.

General Frank Merrill also saw right off that Father Stuart had great rapport with the Kachins, the best fighters in Burma. So the general tried to keep the ubiquitous missionary near his headquarters as much as possible. Shortly before his own death General Merrill wrote: "Father Stuart was the bravest man I ever met."

When Martha Sawyers arrived in Bhamo to do a pastel portrait of Father Stuart, I was living there in a deserted Buddhist monastery high up on the banks of the Irrawaddy. Soon after meeting the missionary she wrote to her editor at *Collier's*: "I had heard fabulous stories of Father Stuart for weeks at various points throughout India and Burma, until he became a huge, towering mythological giant shrouded in mystery. When I met him in Bhamo to draw his portrait I was bowled over by his personal appearance. Instead of the character that I had expected, here was a short, stocky man with a handsome Irish face that was almost too good looking. His voice was quiet, well-modulated in tone, but he could hardly open his mouth without saying something clever, ridiculous, or just plain funny."

Just outside the monastery door, in a courtyard lined with statues of the Buddha, Martha Sawyers settled down to make a sketch of Father Stuart. After a few minutes she said, "You are a man of few words."

"Yes, but I use them over and over."

"How did you happen to become a priest?"

"The police said that I could either go to jail or to the seminary."

Asked a question he could not answer, he explained, "I don't know everything. You see, I was put through the seminary on an incomplete burse."

In time he warmed up enough to tell the artist that Merrill's Marauders had taken up a collection to help finance his church in the Kachin hills. "I'm an Irishman by birth, but I have gotten so much from Americans that I have become an American by 'extraction.'"

After completing the portrait, which included the dashing Aussie hat, the artist held it toward her subject for his inspection. He studied it critically and mused, "No doubt I contributed to the beauty of it."

Martha Sawyers then made a quick pencil sketch of me and dated it May 6, 1945. While she was at it, James Stuart took off toward the Irrawaddy River. It was the last time I was to see him.

At war's end Father Stuart was appointed an officer of the Most Excellent Order of the British Empire for helping the refugees. Later the United States War Department awarded him the Medal of Freedom for his work in saving lives.

During his visit to the States he was much interviewed by the press. A reporter asked, "Who in this country would you most like to meet?" He answered, "Ginger Rogers."

The story went out over the wire, and after having read it Miss Rogers sent the missionary a note saying that when he came to California she would be honored to meet him.

On the plane to Los Angeles, an airlines stewardess asked Father Stuart, who had a way of looking lost, what was his final destination. He showed her an address and asked which bus he might take to get there.

"Don't take a bus," said the stewardess, "take a taxi."

"And where might I find a taxicab?" he asked meekly.

"When you get outside the terminal turn right."

"Are you sure the taxicabs will be there?"

The stewardess kept reassuring him that everything would turn out all right.

When the plane rolled to a stop, a high-school band struck up "When Irish Eyes Are Smiling." There stood Pat O'Brien, who had entertained troops in Burma. And John Ford, the film director, an admirer of the OSS. And Ginger Rogers!

In the midst of the commotion the stewardess worked her way into the crowd until she was close enough to hiss in Father Stuart's ear: "You and your taxicabs!"

Thirty years later when I was doing research in the Columban Fathers' archives in Killiney, I came upon a photograph that startled me. It showed a missionary, Father James Feighery, crossing a stream in Burma astride an animal that had the fine, compact conformation of an army mule. The mule looked familiar.

I went downstairs and mentioned this to Father James Devine, an old Burma hand, explaining that I had gone to Burma because I had volunteered to run mule-trains through the jungle to supply Merrill's Marauders. Alas, by the time I arrived supplies were being air-dropped and mules were no longer needed. Since the mules arrived on a later ship I never knew what had happened to them.

"I can tell you," said Father Devine. "I heard that such animals could be had for the asking. So I sent my catechist on a two-day journey through the jungle to see a sergeant who was trying to find a good home for them. I could have had forty, but the catechist said that ten would be sufficient. I gave them to missionaries in the Kachin hills."

Father Devine asked, "What did you do after learning that mules were redundant?"

I told him I had been assigned to ride herd on fifty-seven war correspondents. That juxtaposition of assignments always amused Father Stuart. He used to ask if I found much difference between mules and correspondents, and I would say I preferred the mules.

Father Stuart is dead, Father Devine told me. He is buried in the cemetery at the Columban Fathers' seminary in County Meath. The hardships of war and years in the jungle took their toll. Even when he made the trip to the United States in 1947, and then went on to visit his home in Ireland, it did not help much. Upon his return to Burma it was evident that he was driving himself; his old vitality was gone. He returned home in 1955 on sick leave, knowing in his heart that he would never go back to Burma. He died suddenly on August 11.

I went out to County Meath and stood at the grave. According to the dates on the stone he had died at age forty-six. The miracle was that he had lived that long. I recalled the day he threw himself onto the floor of a bamboo hut just as bullets tore through the back of the cane chair on which he had been sitting. And the time he flattened himself against a tree as machine-gun slugs chewed away the bark on each side.

Were the situation reversed, and had he stood at my grave, I know what he would have said. Whenever he spoke of someone's death, he always said, "Ah yes, he has gone to where the comfort is."

·3·

An Improbable Beginning

When I met Archbishop Harold Henry, thirty years after meeting Father James Stuart, it was evident right off that he, too, was a colorful character. Did the Saint Columban's Foreign Mission Society specialize in such? Did it have an improbable beginning? Were there signs of the providential from the very start?

Sure enough, in the archives in Killiney, I learned that the Mission Society had a beginning that was highly unusual. It was every bit as improbable as my being asked to write a biography of an archbishop in Korea.

The good seed was planted in Ireland, in 1911, when Father John M. Fraser, a Canadian, arrived from Chekiang, China. He tried with small success to interest the priests and bishops of Ireland in the plight of China. The one thing he did, though, that was destined to bear fruit was give a talk to the students at Maynooth College.

"Of the effect of that lecture at Maynooth I can speak with personal knowledge," Father John Blowick wrote a half-century later. "It brought before the future priests of Ireland the fact that there was still on earth a large nation which was practically altogether pagan, and many were the heart searchings that followed the lecture among the more serious-minded men who had heard it. And even among priests to whom accounts of it had been given during the long summer vacation which followed."

That Father Fraser effectively planted the seed was a mystery to everyone who had met him. He was such an unlikable fellow with a cold, severe manner and an abrasive voice. Not an ounce of charisma seemed in him.

When ready to return to China he decided to travel by way of the United States collecting funds for the French Vincentians working in the Orient.

In New York he was invited to dine with Monsignor James McEnroe and his assistant, Father Edward Galvin, at Holy Rosary rectory in Brooklyn.

At the close of the meal the missionary from China asked the monsignor if he might speak to the parishioners at all of the Masses on Sunday.

"You may not!"

The blunt answer shocked Father Galvin. It puzzled him, for the monsignor was usually a gracious and generous man with any guest who came to the house.

To ease the blow Father Galvin asked the visitor if he would come to his room for a talk. He did not find this easy for he was already seeing Father Fraser as a remote, intense man, with a harsh and monotonous voice.

After the guest was seated on the only chair in the room, Father Galvin sat on the bed and began by saying he had long wanted to be a missionary in China. Even though his guest punctuated everything with disparaging remarks, Ned Galvin felt compelled to tell the highlights of his thirty years of existence from the day he was born in County Cork.

As a boy he had talked of becoming a missionary but was discouraged by parents, friends, pastor and bishop. Go to Maynooth, they said, it is the best seminary in Ireland. He accepted the advice even though he knew that Maynooth prepared priests for work in Ireland and not for foreign missions.

Something unusual happened when Edward Galvin was ordained in 1909: The bishop of Cork had no vacancies in his diocese, the first time that had ever happened. Go to America, the bishop advised, and come back in three years.

The three years were up, Father Galvin told Father Fraser. He had spent many of those days reading books about China in the Brooklyn Public Library. Would the missionary take him along on his return to China?

With cold manner and dead voice, Father Fraser said: "If you want to go with me you'll have to hurry. I'll be leaving in a few weeks. Get permission from your bishop."

What a dreary trip to China! Father Fraser would not permit the young priest to speak with strangers and offered little by way of conversation himself. And even though Ned Galvin had money of his own, the missionary kept him on a near-starvation diet. No tipping was allowed on the long train ride across Canada and on the long voyage across the Pacific. At times when the severe missionary slept the priest from Cork cried with loneliness.

Upon arriving in China, in mid-April of 1912, Father Fraser turned the young priest over to the French Vincentians and disappeared with scarcely a good-bye. The missionaries spoke only Chinese and French, and since Galvin spoke no Chinese and little French he faced still more lonely days.

Every step brought new discouragement, and yet Ned Galvin felt this was the place meant for him. In writing long letters home from China he was being more effective than he knew; the letters were read and reread and passed along and printed in newspapers throughout the country. They helped awaken Ireland to an enthusiasm for the missions.

Father Galvin met two Maynooth priests at Christmas of 1915, when they arrived at the port of Shanghai. While still standing on the hectic dock they told him that his letters had helped them decide to become missionaries, and they urged him to go back home and start a mission society.

Upon returning to Ireland wherever Galvin went he heard the name of John Blowick. He was intrigued by the thought that the brilliant scholar, who at twenty-six held a chair in theology at Maynooth, was willing to turn his back on all of that academic security to become a missionary in China. He must meet him.

Blowick was anxious to meet Galvin, too. Here was an Irish priest, a Maynooth man, who had spent four years in China—surely he would have some suggestions.

When they eventually met by the soft light of a gas lamp, at the front door of a friend's home, they sized up each other. What a contrast! Blowick, small and elegant, almost delicate, dressed in a well-fitting coat and a high top hat. Galvin, big and roughhewn, in a rumpled suit, a too-large Roman collar and cap—only his shoes were polished, as they always were. Father Galvin later described the contrast as ranging "from the ridiculous to the sublime."

The two men had hardly settled in front of the fire in the parlor when they discovered a startling coincidence: Both had been inspired by Father John Fraser. And what an unlikable man!

When Blowick recalled Fraser's lecture at Maynooth that caused so many young men to become interested in mission work, Galvin said, "The strange thing is that he can't stand a mission himself. He spends all the time traveling, recruiting, raising funds, organizing, almost anything but living on the mission. Yet here we are tonight talking about a mission to China because of him."

The more they talked the more they were appalled at the thought of all that would have to come to pass before anyone could so much as pack a trunk for China. The mission society would need to build a seminary, staff it, prepare a program of studies suitable for men destined for the Orient and, of course, raise funds to finance it all.

Even more difficult might be getting the backing of the bishops of Ireland and the approval of the authorities in Rome. What if all of them thought this sounded like a wild-eyed scheme?

By dawn the two priests were talking about a meeting of the bishops of Ireland scheduled for Maynooth five weeks hence. A request should be presented to them.

After some to-do the bishops approved the request. If you get the approval of Rome, they said, you may start a mission house to train priests for China.

Father Blowick sent the proper forms to Rome and the long wait began. Nine months passed and no word. Blowick, a canonist, had some feeling for how Rome took the long view of centuries; Galvin, however, always aware of minutes passing, was beside himself with frustration.

Even though German submarines threatened everything afloat, growing impatience sent the two priests sailing for Rome in June of 1917. Ned Galvin was pessimistic all of the way, saying that even if they received approval for their plan, they would not be assigned favorable territory in China. "They will save that for the Italian missionaries."

The two priests were in Rome a week before receiving an appointment with Cardinal Serafini, prefect for the Congregation of the Propagation of the Faith, and two weeks before being granted an audience with Pope Benedict XV.

During these meetings it was evident that Father Blowick had a sense of diplomacy and that Father Galvin knew a great deal about China. Galvin seemed familiar with every mission in the Orient and with the status of every town. He refused to consider starting missions in remote mountain areas that were full of bandits, suspicion and anti-foreign hatred.

Father Galvin told Pope Benedict that religious orders were trying to hold onto many sections with too few priests. The time has come, he said, to divide those sections and staff them with young men.

The day after the papal audience, June 18, 1917, Cardinal Serafini wrote a letter to Cardinal Logue in Ireland saying that permission is granted for "a college to be founded in Ireland for Foreign Missions."

In Ireland the word China began appearing in the press and flying from mouth to mouth as never before. In county after county young men were expressing a wish to become missionaries.

Father Galvin sailed for the United States on a darkened liner with guns mounted on the foredeck. His friends, and especially his mother, feared he might be a victim of U-boats, for this was November of 1917 and the United States had been at war with Germany since April.

The Irish priest received some encouragement from John Cardinal Farley in New York, William Cardinal O'Connell in Boston, George Cardinal Mundelein in Chicago, and Archbishop John Glennon in Saint Louis. But not one of them could see his way clear to invite another missionary society into his archdiocese.

On Saint Patrick's Day, 1918, Father Galvin arrived in Omaha and thought, as he walked to the episcopal residence, how fitting it would be if on this day the new society could find a new home in the United States. That is exactly what happened when Archbishop Jeremiah J. Harty expressed pleasure at the thought of having missionaries open a headquarters in his diocese.

After all that rejection, at last Ned Galvin felt accepted. With less than $300 in his pocket he hurried down the street to rent a one-room office, hire a sign painter to letter on the door The Irish Mission to China, and locate a printer for his new magazine, *The Far East*.

In April of 1918 Rome made an offer of a mission territory in China— the vicariate of Kweinchow. Galvin replied with a firm rejection: too many mountains, too few people, and too remote.

The official birthday of the society came on June 29, 1918, when Bishop O'Dea of Galway canonically erected the Maynooth Mission to China. Twenty priests took the oath of membership that day.

The Society was making headway in Ireland and in America, and now began directing attention to Australia and New Zealand. Encouraging letters from the bishops of Maitland and Wellington made it clear that priests would be welcome there to prepare young men for China.

During all of this, a strange silence emanating from Rome got on the nerves of priests eager to be on the way. The Society waited with impatience from April of 1918, when the offer to Kweinchow was refused, until November of 1919, when Rome offered the city of Hanyang and some surrounding countryside.

Galvin said he would prefer Hankow across the river. Yet he made no point of this officially when he and Blowick hurried to Rome to accept the offer.

On Saint Patrick's Day of 1920 a farewell party was held at Dalgan, in County Galway, and two days later eleven priests sailed for the mission in China.

Fifty-four years later I sat in the archives in Killiney feeling both pleased and uneasy. After learning the improbable way the Columbans had their beginning, and having known the unlikely Father Stuart in Burma and the rare Archbishop Henry from Korea, the assignment gave little promise of predictability. And yet it should be filled with serendipity. And perhaps the providential.

·4·

Harold Henry Remembers

I went to Korea to visit Archbishop Harold Henry in mid-January of 1975. While waiting for customs to inspect my baggage in Seoul, a well-dressed American, about forty-five years old, came up and started a conversation. I readily answered all of his questions about why I was in Korea, believing that they sprang from a curious and affable nature. Later I learned that he was probably a CIA agent who was somehow affiliated with the intelligence agency of South Korea.

Several things aroused that suspicion. For one thing, he ran a pig farm on Cheju Island, an improbable cover if ever there was one. Another suspicious thing is that he spoke broken Korean when sober, but was remarkably fluent in that tongue when drunk. On one occasion, when drunk, he packed a pistol in his suitcase with such carelessness that it was evident, glinting there on top of the shirts, when airport security opened his luggage. Immediately the security agent snapped shut the bag and nervously waved the American toward a waiting plane.

That would arouse suspicion anywhere, but especially in Korea where security is severe. Whenever I traveled there I was checked three times at the airport—twice within the building and once at the foot of the boarding ramp; that final check was by an agent who knew that if the plane were highjacked he would be executed, and so he frisked with undue vigor. Three guns rode every plane: The pilot carried one, the steward another, and seated somewhere amid the passengers an agent carried the third. The spirit of an armed camp prevailed in South Korea out of a well-founded fear of North Korea.

As I came out of customs two young Columbans greeted me, saying that Archbishop Henry had sent them. The three of us flew to Cheju, an island seventy miles long and forty-five wide, off the southern coast of Korea.

The archbishop was at the airport. As he approached down the long corridor, each step seemed an agony. He looked much older than his sixty-five years. He had declined since our meeting at Notre Dame nine months earlier. I suppose it was the hard life of a missionary that left its mark on a once handsome, athletic man. A magazine writer had described him as having "a soldierly look and something of the air of concentrated, swiftly directed vitality often seen in all-conference quarterbacks."

In a Corona compact we lurched over unpaved streets to a two-story red brick house. The episcopal residence, recently designed by two Columbans, was inexpensive but of good architecture, with its wide-running balconies and sliding doors framing the eminence of Mount Halla. Inside a walled garden the landscaping was the gift of Korean Catholics who had in one day set out nearly two thousand bushes, flowers, plants and trees.

The first thing the archbishop did after showing me to my bright room was to put in a phone call to the States to assure my wife that I had arrived safely. Making that call and having two priests greet me at Seoul reflected the thoughtfulness that had made Harold Henry revered in South Korea.

After the confining hours on the plane I felt a need for exercise, and so one of the young priests took me for a wintery walk. Two hundred yards from the archbishop's residence we came upon an outdoor market that was set up there on a windswept field once a week. The scene could date back a thousand years—it reflected no sophistication, just human nature without any sugar coating. Two rows of facing tents were surrounded by seething crowds of people with Mongolian features, a reminder that Genghis Khan used to winter his troops on Cheju. The troops had a battle cry: "Where we ride the grass will never grow again!" Descendants of their tough little ponies were now pulling crude wooden carts around the marketplace. A blanket, stretching between pony and cart, served as a manure catcher. My guide explained that this is conservation: The manure serves as fertilizer, and so the land feeds the pony and the pony feeds the land.

The next morning when I went down to breakfast I found Archbishop Henry on his hands and knees in the living room cleaning up a mess the dog had made on the carpet. Although Maria, the maid, was in the next room he completed the task himself.

At ten o'clock the archbishop came to my room to begin a long series of interviews. He was surprised that I had found in the archives in Killiney several letters he had written at age thirteen to the superior general of the Columbans, for he had long forgotten them. And, of course, he was not aware of letters the Columbans had written about him during his years in the seminary, and was pleased to find them favorable.

He asked where to begin and I suggested that he start recalling his boyhood and life in the seminary, beginning from the day of birth and continuing on until his arrival in Korea.

So he began by saying that he was born July 11, 1909, in Northfield, Minnesota. He was baptized in the Moravian Church, and for a reason he could not explain he became fiercely anti-Catholic at an early age.

"I believed that the Catholic priests had sinister powers and could put the 'double whammy' on me. In Northfield I used to cross the street when passing St. Dominic's, the very church in which I would eventually say my first solemn Mass."

Harold's mother died when he was ten, and his father soon married a Catholic widow with three grown daughters. One of them, Isobel, told Harold to quit flitting from school to school; he had attended seven public schools in six years because his father, a mechanic, had flitted from job to job. She suggested that the boy settle down at St. Stephen's, a parochial school in Minneapolis, and she sold the idea by promising that there he could play football. At this point in the story the archbishop said to me, "Isobel must have had her fingers crossed because there was no football played in that school."

Archbishop Henry said that he had agreed to give St. Stephen's a try under condition that he did not have to become a Catholic. Here again, as the poster on the convent wall in Tokyo says, "The starting-points of human destiny are little things." The parochial school probably did not set the direction of his life as much as a magazine that his stepsister subscribed to—*The Far East*, published by the Columban Fathers. It was filled with stories about China, stories that the boy found fascinating. And the pictures! Pagodas, rickshaws, pagan idols, terraced rice fields, sampans!

At age twelve Harold Henry decided to become a Catholic. His baptism was informal, sort of all of a sudden, because he wanted to make his First Communion with the other children in May of 1922. One morning his teacher, Sister Mary, told him to go over to the church during the lunch hour so that Father Gaughan might baptize him. She knew that St. Stephen's was playing a baseball game that afternoon, and so she ignored the fact that Harold wore a uniform and spikes. He thoughtfully removed his spikes at the vestibule before entering the church, little realizing how much coming events cast their shadows before: As a priest he would build forty-six churches and their vestibules would be filled with a clutter of shoes,

and he would, out of deference to custom, remove his shoes before entering any Korean home, even his own rectory.

The Far East magazine inspired Harold's interest in the priesthood. He
was forever quoting it to his father, describing the exciting lives that missionaries lead. No doubt he saw it all as a great adventure.

At breakfast one morning, three months after the baptism, Harold's
father pointed to a notice in *The Far East* that said the Columban Fathers
would accept at their new preparatory seminary in Omaha any bright boy
who had finished the seventh grade. Harold, never one to dally, got off a
letter before lunch.

Harold Henry was baptized, made his First Communion, was confirmed
and began studying for the priesthood all within these months. He studied
in Omaha and later at St. Senan's on the River Shannon, and at Dalgan
Park in County Galway.

Perhaps the greatest influence in the boy's life was Father Timothy Harris, a teacher in the seminary. For example, one day Father Harris, in a sermon on the proper use of creature comforts, urged as a guiding principle
St. Ignatius's admonition: "If you have the good things of life enjoy them
and thank God for them. If you don't have them, don't complain." Harold
Henry would quote that often during the next fifty years.

At breakfast, the morning after the sermon on the proper use of creature
comforts, the soft-boiled eggs seemed barely to have touched warm water.
The eggs at St. Senan's were repulsive to begin with; the chickens ate wild
garlic growing around the college grounds and so flavored their product that
it was best if one thought of something else while eating them. The boys left
the breakfast table disgruntled with the barely boiled eggs untouched in the
cups.

During the sermon an hour later Father Harris said: "We prepared those
eggs that way this morning on purpose. I wanted to see what you had learned
about the proper use of creature comforts. Not much. I can't say that I am
surprised, but I am disappointed."

Then he told them how in the days of the classic Chinese society, when
someone asked, "How do you do?" the answer was not the mindless, "Very
well, thank you!" but the thoughtful, "I am trying to remedy my grave
defects, but so far without success." Father Harris urged the seminarians at
least to make a try at remedying their grave defects.

Since Harold Henry could not afford to return to the States for any holi-
days, members of the faculty took turns seeing to it that he was not lonely.
For instance, Father John McFadden took Harold to visit two uncles and

two aunts who lived in a whitewashed cottage with thatched roof halfway up a hill. Picturesque it was, but comfortable it was not. There was no running water. The aunts had to carry heavy buckets from the spring at the foot of the hill. "When Father John discovered an artesian well atop the hill," Archbishop Henry told me, "he took a few of the pound notes tucked away behind the picture frame and bought some pipe for a sink. All during the digging and pipe-laying Uncle Michael kept objecting, 'John, we'll be the laughing stock of the neighborhood with water coming into the house.' When Father John and I left, the uncle moved the sink outside. He would bring it back into the house whenever he heard his nephew was planning a visit."

Harold Henry admitted that a love of sports always loomed large in his life. He told me that had he not gone to Ireland to study he probably would never have reached the priesthood because the sports program that he needed to keep up his morale did not exist at the Columban seminaries in Omaha, Nebraska, and Silver Creek, New York.

In Ireland he discovered rugby and gloried in it. His speed and aggressiveness caused so many injuries that the authorities at the seminary told him either to tone down or be banished from the playing field. During vacations he went to Wales with a fellow student who had relatives there and played for the Wales Rugby Union under the name of Ivor Thomas. "I found the Welsh miners tougher than I was," he recalled. "They'd kick you in the ribs when the referee wasn't looking. The student who took me to Wales died when a rib punctured his lung."

While in the seminary, Harold was eager for every bit of news he could get out of China, especially the letters Bishop Galvin sent back to Ireland. From my research in Killiney I knew that during the floods, in an avalanche of despair, Bishop Galvin had written: "I have never encountered such desperate people as the people who are camping out here on the hillside. Hunger has made them desperate. I am honestly afraid to go out. Every time I do they catch on to my clothes. They hold on for dear life until I promise them something. I cannot feed everyone. We are now feeding 900—a drop in the ocean. It is estimated that there are thirty million homeless in the Yangtze Valley and most of them have absolutely nothing. I never knew what 'nothing' meant until I came to China. Poverty is hard, but hunger is terrible. And the Communists? My God, what demons they are! Robbing and killing right and left. They have taken the boats from the people and what little they were able to save from the flood. There is no money anywhere. Every single one of our missions has been attacked and looted. No one has escaped."

In another of Bishop Galvin's letters, which I read aloud to the archbishop, came the terrible sentence, "Flesh and blood can't stand the strain
we are under here." And it added, "I think our Society ought to look for
some other field in which to work."

"That's the sentence that changed my life!" said Archbishop Henry so
suddenly that I was startled. "That is the one that did it!"

Before our interview had progressed an hour I felt a certain elation, knowing for sure that the archbishop would supply me with an abundance of
anecdotes. All of his life he had been a raconteur. Having repeated stories
so often through the years he kept them from being dulled by the passing
of time.

When the maid rang the gong to announce lunch, I noticed that Harold
Henry had grown more youthful during the past two hours. Although his
lungs, legs and heart were less than effective, each morning from ten until
twelve the same thing happened: He became younger looking while recalling the adventures of the past. It was uncanny. I have since wished that I
had taken a photograph of him at the start of an interview and another at
the end of it to see if the change would show on film.

·5·

Adaptation Totale in Korea

China beckoned to Harold Henry through boyhood and early youth. His daydreams focused on that exotic land; his letters told of his hope to do missionary work there. When I came to know the archbishop, he still believed that his desire for China was a providential beckoning that led him to Catholicism and to the priesthood.

Upon receiving an appointment to China, in September 1933, he read and reread the letter. Every now and then he would say, "China," as though it were the most beautiful word in the world.

En route there the steamship *President Jefferson* stopped at Kobe, Japan. Father Henry, age twenty-four, stood at the rail enjoying his first sight of an Oriental port. The purser brought him a letter and right then the bottom fell out of his high hopes and bright plans. He was not to go to China after all. Go to Korea, the letter directed, the Columbans are opening a mission there.

The young priest turned to the woman standing next to him at the rail and asked, "Where in the world is Korea?"

"Aside from shock, what else was your reaction?" I asked.

"When I read that letter I accepted it," he said. "I had taken the oath of obedience and that was that! If such happened today, a priest might call a press conference, leave the Church and write a book.

"But I can see now it was for the best. The Providence of God is remarkable. I could never have made a go of it in China. Bandits, floods, Communists spitting in your face. I couldn't have taken it."

He could have taken it all right, of that I am sure. He bore the afflictions of Korea so well that surely he would have survived with grace those of China. Each day I was in Cheju I came to see him more and more as a living example of the Greek philosopher's observation: Your character is your fate. At the core of his character was the instant response to any problem: "No sweat!" Fate seemed determined to test that attitude, and so the recurring theme of his life was trouble after trouble.

Right off, Korea put to a test Harold Henry's optimism. The immediate problems were language, customs and food.

A Korean priest, Father Pak, was supposed to teach him the language. The fragile old man met the vigorous young Columban at the railroad station and they set off by a steaming Model T taxi that stopped often to take on water. The path became too narrow for the Ford a mile from the church, and so the two priests walked the rest of the way to remote Noan.

Father Pak, unfamiliar with English, conversed in Latin. Eventually he hired a Korean boy to come to the rectory for an hour each evening to help the American with a most difficult language.

Eager Harold Henry wanted to call each parishioner by name but was confronted by one of many unfamiliar customs: Each had several names. Koreans believe that the name given at birth will influence a child's destiny and so they give such names as Gentle Heart, Prosperous Old Age, Many Talents, Increased Happiness, Spring Fragrance, and Bright Jade. Soon after getting this "fate name" the child gets a nickname, often uncomplimentary, a carry-over from the Chinese belief that spirits try to infect the best-loved child; so parents try to fool the spirits with such names as Stupid Dog, Bed Bug, Poor Potato. In school there is a book name. Later a business or professional name. And, if baptized, a Christian name.

Food led to digestive problems for the young priest who up until then had an unshakable stomach. A woman cooked for Father Pak, but the pastor hired Peter to cook Western style for his American assistant. It was evident that Peter had not the slightest idea of what Western food was like. Father Henry, no chef himself, tried to teach him the fundamentals, stressing aesthetics since Peter had a genius for making food seem repulsive.

One day—glory be!—Peter served a dish of fish, potatoes and cabbage looking so attractive that it deserved to be photographed for the jacket of a cookbook. But the taste! To show appreciation for the great visual improvement, Father Henry tried to force himself to eat it. Finally, he pushed the plate aside and said, "I can't eat this. What did you do with it?" Peter answered, "You Americans don't like the hot spicy food we eat in Korea. So I put sugar on everything." For the rest of his life Harold Henry avoided sugar, even in coffee.

In time, the young Columban told his superior, "My stomach is killing me. Peter will be the death of me. Father Pak won't fire him because he says he is a good and holy man." The superior observed, "As Aristotle would say, holiness in a cook is a purely accidental quality."

Harold Henry knew that the hardest thing to achieve would be what the French missionaries called *adaptation totale*. He must cease being a stranger in a strange land and try to see life as Koreans see it, to react and feel as they do. He would never be able to bring this off completely because he looked at life through a template formed long ago in Greece and Rome, altered somewhat by a Judeo-Christian culture and an Anglo-Saxon heritage. In time, though, he would adapt so totally that he would be admired by Orientals and Occidentals alike.

As a new missionary he had expected problems with language, culture and food but had not foreseen the Thought Control Police. His relationship with them grew more uneasy with the years until eventually the police put him in prison.

When he complained to Father Pak about the way the police questioned him, the old man explained that ever since 1910, when Korea became a colony of Japan, police interrogations were a part of the Korean way of life. Be nice to those fellows, Father Pak warned, or they will make life miserable for you. During the next nine years Harold Henry often recalled those words.

One time when the young Columban was hearing confessions a member of the Thought Control Police asked an old lady what the American was up to. To impress him she said that the *sin-bu-nim* was listening to what people had done wrong, and that even though threatened by death he would never reveal what he had heard. This got the policeman so excited that he said he must sit in the confessional right next to the priest. Although Father Henry was able to scotch this plan, the policeman was so disturbed that he kept sucking on his teeth, in the Japanese manner, for the rest of the day.

When told to start the first Columban parish in Korea, Father Henry's heart skipped a few beats. And at Naju of all places! It was a sorry, smelly town—rundown, backward, disheveled. The people there had a bad reputation—tough, stubborn, difficult to deal with.

It had been the capital of a province until, at the time the Japanese took over, somebody assassinated the governor. So, out of spite, the Japanese moved the capital to Kwangju. It was also in Naju, in March 1919, that the student riots against the Japanese started at the railroad station and spread across Korea. From then on the Japanese made sure that nothing nice happened to Naju. The official attitude was: "Let it lie there rotting in the sun."

There Father Henry built a church of orange-crate lumber. It was not exactly a cathedral, the young pastor admitted, but after all only seventeen Catholics lived within walking distance.

Harold Henry, the ingrained optimist, felt disheartened many times during his first year as pastor. He was painfully aware that in an area of half a million people he had only 17 parishioners in Naju church and only 150 scattered throughout the mission stations. He tried repeating to himself something heard in the seminary: "In God's plan some sow and others reap." But he wanted to see a little of the harvest. Right now! He had been getting gready for this since that afternoon in 1922 when the Columbans accepted him for the seminary. That was thirteen years ago!

He often recalled the pastor in Minneapolis who could not understand why anyone would want to be a missionary. The old priest used to say to him, "There is China enough at home!" Maybe he is right, maybe there is Korea enough at home. There is a shortage of priests in the States. Yes, but . . . a providential prompting kept him struggling in Korea.

The young priest soon began to see enough results to feel encouraged. The parish grew from 17 to 100 within two years. Since the little orange-crate church was now inadequate, plans were begun for a new one. Just as Father Henry was wondering where the money would come from, Bishop Cushing, later the cardinal, sent the Columban Fathers $2,500 for a new church. Shabby, disheveled Naju, of scurrying rats and rank sewage, got the money and in time celebrated the dedication of a new church on October 7, 1937.

The people in Naju area seemed hungry for religion. Korea had little to offer. There were some Christians, but they were only a fraction of the population. Buddhism was practically dead there; the temples had become ill-kept museums. Confucianism, imported from China more than a thousand years ago, is more of a code of behavior than a religion, although Confucius did say: "He who does not recognize a Divine Law cannot be a superior man." Shamanism, the religion that Father Henry came upon most often, worships spirits inhabiting sun, moon, earth, mountains, rivers, trees.

The Thought Control Police did not know they were driving people toward the missionaries. "It was during this time," the archbishop told me, "that I realized why the Koreans are called the Irish of the East. They have a deep faith, a sense of humor, and are usually against any government that tries to tell them what to do."

After eight years he was beginning to feel at home. Now he could look at

Koreans without being aware of their high cheek bones, noses flattened at the bridge, and Mongoloid eyefolds. They, in turn, could talk with him without focusing attention on the size of his feet or the length of his nose, and they no longer asked how he liked Korea or commented on his mastery of the language.

Still he felt a need to get away from time to time to be with other Columbans. He would get hungry for spoken English and for talk about the green hills of home, the World Series and the Notre Dame football season. The hunger would lessen with the years, but he realized one cannot arrive in the East as late as age twenty-four and shake off the West in all ways.

So in early December 1941 he asked the police in Naju for permission to visit his fellow Columbans in Mokpo. Upon reaching the mission headquarters he fell into a daily routine, part of which was listening to the evening news on the radio. The broadcasts were in Japanese even though the station was located in Mokpo. Father Joseph O'Brien, pastor of the tiny Japanese church next door, was translator.

One evening just as Monsignor Owen MacPolin, Father Henry and Father O'Brien settled down in the monsignor's office for the newscast, the announcer exploded onto the air in a frenzy. A shadow fell across Father O'Brien's face. He seemed reluctant to translate. Finally he said, "They bombed Pearl Harbor."

He continued translating: "The United States fleet has been destroyed. . . . The American imperialists have committed untold crimes against the Japanese. . . . The imperialists have long interfered with the prosperity of the Far East."

Just as the fifteen-minute newscast was ending, there came a loud banging on the door. Five Korean policemen led by a Japanese officer burst into the house and pinned Harold Henry against the wall in the hallway. They marched nine Columbans down a steep hill and lined them up in front of Chief Morinaga at the Mokpo police station.

After a tirade, Chief Morinaga ended on a note of sadness: "Americans must be punished and yet we must protect you. That is our duty. You must stay here. The accommodations are not the best. What do you think of that?"

"If it is all right with you," said the monsignor, "I would rather go back to my house and take my chances."

"Do you want to die?" screamed the chief of police, pointing toward the street. Outside a crowd chanted for the death of all Americans. Mokpo was thirty percent Japanese and a good many of them had rushed to the police station to start a demonstration the minute the newscast ended.

"Most of us are Irish," said the monsignor.

"But they can't tell you from Americans," yelled the chief.

"But we are neutral."

"Yes, you are neutral. But you are neutral on the wrong side."

The Columbans were herded into a cell. Father Henry saw that if he stretched out his arms he could touch both sides, so it was about six feet long and nine wide, a tight fit for nine men and an oval wooden box that served as a toilet. After stumbling about in the dark, and some bumps and bruises, the priests found that if each lay on his side and did not shift or turn, they could fit.

The rule of enforced silence accentuated the sounds of torture down the hall. With each thud and scream and groan, Father Henry suffered double agony, one for the victim down the hall and one out of fear that at any moment he, the American, would be given like treatment.

After a few days he was returned under guard to Naju for interrogation by Chief Honda of the Thought Control Department. The questioning went on for days from early morning until late night. Often the Japanese tried to get the prisoner to reveal himself as a spy. For instance, two detectives entered his cell at two o'clock in the morning. Although the priest slept on an icy, stone floor with only one blanket as cover, he was able to sleep well after a day of interrogation. A detective shook him awake and said hurriedly, "We have just run out of invisible ink. We need it to send a message. It is very important. Please help us. We know you have some hidden in yout house. Tell us where to find it. We won't hold it against you."

"Invisible ink?" said the sleepy prisoner. "How can you see it if it is invisible?"

The detectives sucked air through their teeth and let Harold Henry go back to sleep.

Near midnight on Christmas Eve, Chief Honda completed reviewing the vast dossier on Harold Henry's activities for the past eight years and said that would be all for the time being. Hardly had the cell door closed behind the missionary than the church bell, the big one he had ordered from France, began to ring for midnight services. It rang louder and longer than usual; Dominic, the cook, was riding the rope to wish his pastor a Merry Christmas.

For another five months Father Henry was a prisoner and then, quite suddenly, he learned that he would be exchanged for Japanese prisoners in the United States. Under guard he was escorted to the rectory to pick up some personal belongings. As he left the house, ready to go to the railroad station, he found the schoolyard filled with children standing in solemn silence. He looked at the Japanese guard and the guard nodded. The pastor started to talk to the children, but after a few sentences broke down. The children were crying too. He realized then that he had come a long way over the rocky road to *adaptation totale.*

·6·

Years of War

At the time I lived in the archbishop's residence early in 1975, the bitterness of Vietnam still clung to the national palate. Anyone who had taken part in any war felt uneasy mentioning it, for the quickest way to become a pariah was to speak of having served in the military. So when Harold Henry began telling of his wartime experiences he was pleased to know I had served in the Second World War and in the Korean conflict. He could speak freely and at length, knowing I would understand what he did and why he did it.

He said that after a hectic voyage on the *Gripsholm*, the neutral Swedish ship that exchanged prisoners, he stepped ashore in New York and immediately expressed a wish to enlist as an army chaplain. His superior refused permission, feeling that the young missionary had been through enough for the time being. When Bishop Cushing of Boston heard about this he was annoyed and made a long-distance call to the superior in Omaha. Then he made another long-distance call and announced, "Hello, Harold, you're in the army now!"

After attending Chaplain's School at Harvard, Father Henry was assigned to a unit of combat engineers that landed in Normandy at Omaha Beach, the most deadly expanse in the invasion of Europe. Following the Saint-Lô breakthrough, the engineers were attached to the XX Corps to serve as a spearhead for General Patton's Third Army.

Once past Saint-Lô, Chaplain Henry's outfit drove for thirty-six hours straight, delayed from time to time by some resistance, but the real resistance did not come until Arnaville, on the Moselle River. There the unit worked all night to build a pontoon bridge while Patton's infantrymen and tanks crowded up for miles waiting to cross. Things went badly because the Germans, with every square yard zeroed in, could drop an 88-millimeter shell wherever they wanted at any time. They would wait until the bridge was almost finished and down would come a barrage to wipe out all of that effort.

A chemical company eventually fogged the area with smoke. Behind the smoke screen the engineers completed the bridge; troops crossed over and were on the way to Metz, a town never taken by frontal attack.

Metz was surrounded by forts with reinforced concrete walls two yards thick and so sturdy that bombs and shells just chipped away at them with no real damage. The Nazis, with Germanic thoroughness, plotted their positions so that artillery, mortars and crossing machine-gun fire surrounded the city with a shield of death.

General Patton said that if any soldier were killed in a frontal attack on Metz, that soldier's commanding officer would be immediately relieved of command. He gave the order to "run the gauntlet" around Metz and surround it, knowing that when the Germans inside the forts ran out of food they would surrender, as they did.

To run the gauntlet was tricky business, a game of Russian roulette. Vehicles did not dare travel in usual convoy discipline, going at a fixed speed with equal distance between them. They shot across the deadly ground in spurts at varying speeds, anything to make it difficult for German gunners to get a lead on them.

Chaplain Henry and his assistant, Bob Garneau, parked their jeep by a wall. They noticed it could be seen by the enemy, so they moved it. A few minutes later an 88 shell hit the exact spot where the jeep had stood.

During the day Chaplain Henry ran the gauntlet offering Mass at several places along the line. At night he would stay with the engineers wherever they were building, for the river crossings were the most dangerous operations. The engineers first threw across a footbridge for the infantry, cleared mines for the spearhead and blew up pillboxes. Next they built a more substantial bridge across the same river to get the tanks into action.

It was in one such operation that Chaplain Henry was decorated with the Bronze Star for valor.

The archbishop told me that the thing he found most difficult was writing to parents to tell them about the death of a son. "I often think about the parents of soldiers," he said. "The valor we ask of them! I feel the same way about the parents of missionaries. Nobody talks about the sacrifice they make. The missionary is engrossed in his work, he doesn't have time to fret about his lot. But the folks back home think about him living in mud huts, in danger, eating poor food. They worry."

One day Chaplain Henry was looking for one of the bath units that General Patton insisted the service engineers erect behind the front lines the moment there was a pause in forward movement. While lurching across the rutted road in Luxembourg, the Columban anticipated the creature comforts that Father Harris used to speak of in the seminary—a hot shower and a hot meal. He recalled the admonition that when you have them enjoy them, but when you don't have them don't complain.

Suddenly Generals Patton, Walker and Irwin loomed in front of him. General Patton, whom he had met several times before, waved him to a halt. He wanted to know where the bridge was being built for the tanks. Chaplain Henry said, "I just came from there. About a mile down the road you come to a fork. Be sure you stay to the right. To the left there's nothing but Germans."

"Thank you, Padre," said Patton, "I appreciate this. It wouldn't pay to be caught by the Germans, would it?"

The next time he met Patton the general was paying off a debt. He had promised that if a bridge were completed by a certain deadline he would give the combat engineers a case of whiskey. The engineers made the deadline and Patton kept his promise. In the course of the conversation on that occasion, Patton said to Harold Henry, "Padre, you're a goddam fine chaplain!"

At the end of the war Harold Henry was itchy to get back to Korea. But everywhere he went he was told that civilians were not permitted to return to Korea: The situation there was too "unstable," a vague word much used in bureaucracy. Finally, he did what he had been doing all of his life—he went to the top: His letter to the Joint Chiefs of Staff was such a masterpiece in salesmanship that it got him a ride on a troop ship to Inchon.

He arrived amid rumors of how trouble was brewing now that the country was divided in half. He paid no attention, feeling that there are always prophets of doom throwing dark shadows across life. Certainly he was not prepared to believe that within three years the Columbans would suffer in Korea more severely than they had during the Second World War.

At the moment he suffered a severe attack of homesickness. He had come to accept the soft life of the States without realizing it. In facing the burdens of a new assignment he had to keep in mind the things Father Harris had said in the seminary: You have to be open-minded to God's will and willing to be led; those are conditions of divine guidance.

His new burden was more than he had anticipated. First off, he was startled to see the changes five years had brought to Monsignor MacPolin, who at sixty looked much older. There was a sagging in the features and in the spirit that had not been there before, not even during those days in the crowded cell in Mopko.

The monsignor said he would be returning to Ireland; he had been in Korea for fourteen years and before that in China for eight. Father Henry would be in charge of the Korean mission until his return.

When eventually Harold Henry learned that the monsignor would never return, he wrote him a letter that was not the most charitable he had ever composed. He complained of the sorry state of affairs he inherited: Upon opening the safe he had found less than $100 in Korean money. While it was true that Korea had been cut from the Columban budget during the war, still the war had been over for more than two years and no budget applied for. The Koreans were too poor to support their pastors, who often lacked money for food. Then there were the IOUs that Monsignor MacPolin had signed for food in Kwangju, promising to pay back the debt in rice after the war. Father Henry was determined to redeem the IOUs as soon as possible.

He applied to the Columbans for a budget. He also asked help from Rome and received $12,000 from the request.

"We were certainly grateful to the United States troops in those lean days," said Archbishop Henry. "They knew we didn't have anything, and so they said we were welcome to eat in their mess halls and buy in the PX. The Columbans had acted as interpreters and advisers to the military government and had let the military use their parish facilities, and now they were showing their appreciation."

The optimism that came so naturally to Father Henry was beginning to wane. He wrote to a friend in the States: "Korea has changed considerably —for the worse. It is really in a terrible condition from every point of view. The Communists are busy night and day with their propaganda. They have freedom of activity in the country places where they cannot be watched so closely. The people join the party through fear, dreading the reprisals if they do not. Many Koreans who call themselves Communists are not the atheistic kind. They think that being Communists means they will get the former Japanese land free. The propaganda is sufficiently vague to fool the people and get votes for Communist leaders."

Harold Henry longed to mount his bicycle and go from village to village as in the days before the war, but he was stuck with desk work. One thing he did that brought him satisfaction at this time was to develop a language course for new missionaries. He still cringed at the recollection of the sorry language training he had suffered.

In the States, from the end of the war until his return to Korea, Harold Henry had taken a Berlitz course in French. The same system could be used in teaching Korean, he decided. With his French book in hand he set about adapting the lessons to his needs.

For forty-five minutes each morning he drilled the young priests in one new construction and ten new words. He never permitted them to write down anything, feeling that learning a language is in great part memory, and so they must train the memory to record sounds and retain them. With the Berlitz book as a guide, he composed sentences in Korean and had the students learn expression after expression by rote. Next he held up objects —books, teacup, hat—and had students call out the names. After this brisk warm-up, Father Henry would turn over the class to Gregory Kim who would put the young priests through more subtle paces for the next six hours.

All through 1949 and the early months of 1950 Father Henry's letters were filled with distress: "Police were tied up and killed as well as people who were active anti-Communists. . . . A few bullets hit Father Brandon's bed but he had ducked down. . . . High-school students were given guns, and they set up their own courts and liquidated any students or teachers they did not like or who were expressly anti-Communist."

Despite all of this he was not prepared for the news the morning the young priests came to language class all excited, saying that at dawn the armies of the North Korean Communists had come down across the 38th parallel!

Father Henry told them not to worry, there are always skirmishes up there. They assured him that this was not a skirmish but the real thing. He kept saying, "No, no." He did not want to believe it. There he stood on June 25, 1950, only a few feet from the spot where he had heard the news of Pearl Harbor in 1941. He was not ready to face another war. He had seen enough of rubble to be attracted to the Chinese proverb: "What cannot be made in a hundred years can be spoiled in less than a morning."

Father Henry, with his love of adventure and his attitude of "no sweat," was soon involved in the Korean conflict. Right off he led a convoy of four jeeps filled with missionaries on a 220-mile trip through the Mount Chiri area in which 20,000 Communist Koreans operated. He continued using his war experience to move Columbans from place to place in comparative safety. Seven of his confreres, not under his guidance, were captured and killed by the Communists. The details of their deaths are in a later chapter that tells of all the Columbans who died, through the years, as a result of violence.

·7·

Season of Growth

As the archbishop finished talking about his experience in two wars, he walked toward the French doors, looked toward Mount Halla and said, "Tomorrow we are going to have a rough day." That came as a jolt. Normally his approach to the impossible was, "No sweat!"

He foresaw a rough day ahead of us because the biggest blizzard in Cheju's memory was blowing, blowing, blowing. The snow flew so parallel to the ground that it seemed never to come to rest. To allow such fierce wind to blow through, the stone walls of Cheju are built with chinks in them.

The next day dawned rough for us, all right. The island was one great frozen pond when we started on a two-and-a-half hour trip so that the archbishop might confer the sacrament of confirmation. Our Korean driver had never faced ice before and sped along as though it were a day in June. A few miles out of town he rammed the car into the rear of a truck, badly crumpling the right fender. A curious crowd gathered, cars accumulated behind us, and the two drivers started to fight. I stopped the fight and pulled the fender away from the wheel; Harold Henry popped heart pills into his mouth as though they were peanuts. The driver, learning nothing from the experience, continued to tailgate the rest of the way.

We reached the church just in time for the start of the ceremony. As I stepped out of my shoes in the vestibule, I wondered how I would find them among so many pairs. It was easy, though; they were the only ones size twelve among all those sandals: two ocean liners docked amid a thousand tugboats.

On the return trip I commented on the number of adults confirmed that morning. The archbishop recalled the really large confirmation classes of twenty years earlier. When the Korean war ended in 1953 there were 160,000 Catholics in Korea; ten years later there were 628,000.During those years Harold Henry grew too, as indicated by his rapidly changing titles: He became a monsignor in 1954, a bishop in 1957 and an archbishop in 1962.

"I believe that this outpouring of grace came as a result of the Church's agony on Korean soil," he said. "A sort of reimbursement for suffering. I am not just thinking of the seven Columbans who died. I remember Patrick J. Byrne, a Maryknoll bishop, who died in captivity after the Death March. And that seventy-six-year-old French nun, Sister Beatrice, who was shot on the Death March. Bishop Boniface Sauer, a Benedictine, and one of his German priests died in prison. Twelve priests of the Paris Foreign Mission were killed or died of ill treatment. Bishop Francis Hong disappeared in captivity. Innumerable Catholics and Protestants were killed, died in prison or just disappeared as captives.

"We had more than 400 Catholics who could have saved their lives by denying their faith, but they chose the firing squad instead. It is interesting to note that the majority had been baptized within the previous three years. So the remark, 'They are rice Christians' is not apt there. Rice Christians do not die for their faith. Yes, those of us who survived were reimbursed for such sacrifices, most of which we'll never even know about."

Another reason that religion flourished, Archbishop Henry believed, is that in South Korea the Communists were their own worst enemies. Many Koreans, toying with the idea that maybe Communism offered solutions to the troubles of life, found that the Reds brought more chaos and destruction. As Father Austin Sweeney wrote from Cheju Island: "One thing certainly is clear in all of this mix-up: Communist propaganda will not deceive the people of Cheju again."

Another reason for the amazing growth was the friendship that grew between priests and people during the long agony. The Koreans were impressed that foreign priests shared their anguish when they really did not have to. They were impressed that the poor received help just because they were poor and not for any advantage the giver might receive. Koreans became curious about a Church that gave something for nothing.

Another thing in the Church's favor was the good example set by the United States Army GI. "Young Korean men were attracted to the Church because they saw a high percentage of American soldiers attending services," said Archbishop Henry. "It was quite impressive when you consider that nearly thirty percent of the American troops were Catholic. You might say that all of this gave 'face' to the Church, and nothing can succeed in the Orient without 'face.'"

With "face" the Church attracted more sophisticated Koreans. For generations it had been the "potters' Church." The potters were at the bottom of the social ladder, one step below the butchers. Their ancestors, many of them wealthy men, had fled to southwestern Korea to escape religious persecution a century ago. With the image of Christianity changed, missionaries were approached by judges, teachers, physicians, merchants and military leaders seeking admission into the Church.

Harold Henry was under pressure because so many Koreans wanted to join the Church but there were too few priests to care for them. For example, even his old friend, Father Frank Woods, began putting pressure on him when the parish in Changseng had a deluge of converts. The trickle of the old days grew to a stream and suddenly the stream became a torrent. A village of 1,200 where there were no Catholics begged Father Woods to come to it, or at least send a catechist. A second, larger village sent a deputation making the same request. A third and fourth followed closely on these two.

Father Woods asked Bishop Henry for another priest. He was told, as indeed he already knew, that a priest could not be spared. He next asked for help to employ additional catechists and was told that for lack of money he would have to make do with the catechists he had.

Father Woods passed on the bad news to the four villages. Maybe later, he said, holding out a hope he really did not feel. The villagers refused to wait. If Father Woods could not instruct them, they would do it themselves. And so, after buying a few catechisms, the group leader in each village set about teaching his fellow villagers, learning himself as he went along.

In face of such determination, Father Woods took action. He arranged for the instruction of the group leaders; in two villages he contrived also to have catechism classes held. A simple church, built by voluntary labor on a donated site, went up in one village; a second church was under way in another. At this point five additional villages came along with similar requests. Thousands were clamoring for instruction. Right now! Immediately!.

During that period of rapid growth every Columban felt desperation. How to care for so many with so little! One priest, to provide shelter for his ever-growing flock, sold his shotgun, radio and watch. He thought twice before selling the shotgun because it helped supplement a meager diet. In his pursuit of food, he and other missionaries had learned to disguise themselves as Korean farmers so that they might get close to birds without attracting attention. They wore white coveralls and moved with the slow rhythmic pace of farmers, until ducks, geese or pheasants were properly aligned, and then felled several with a single shot. After selling his shotgun the missionary became a vegetarian.

The burden of administration was especially hard on Harold Henry's morale. Those unending meetings that proliferated in the Church after the Second Vatican Council used to drive him up the wall. He wrote to friends: "I went to the bishops' meeting in Seoul for three consecutive days of hot air all morning and all afternoon. It took me three days to get back to normal."

Meetings and desk work made him restless because the athlete inside him was always eager to be set free. He sometimes paused and stared into space remembering the days he rode a bike from village to village and climbed steep mountain trails to some remote mission station.

Whenever the chafing became too severe he found an excuse to slip away from the chancery office and then, as always, adventure found him. Typhoons, blizzards, wrecks and near-misses seemed to search him out. As an example he wrote to friends in the States: "On the way back we had engine trouble and the fuel pressure warning light was flickering on and off. So the pilot flew along the Nak Dong River so we could land on a sand bank if necessary. We made Taegu and changed planes for a flight over the Chiri Mountains. The pilot, a captain in the ROK army, told us there was no sweat, that he had been shot down twice in Vietnam and succeeded both times in making a forced landing."

The archbishop was always surprised when I recalled such an incident which he had nearly forgotten. I was able to do it because before leaving for Korea I had visited his friends in El Paso and Tucson and they had allowed me to read letters written years ago. As a young priest Harold Henry had sat by candlelight on many a dark Korean night pouring out his heart to friends back home.

·8·

Help People Help Themselves

With all of those problems, at the end of the Korean war, it would seem that Harold Henry would not go out of his way to create new ones, but he did. He wanted hospitals and clinics and schools. When friends looked at him as though he could not possibly be serious, he flaunted his "no sweat" attitude and went ahead and raised the money to build buildings and somehow enticed the staffs to run the institutions.

His most haunting question: How to help these people help themselves? He did not approve of unending handouts. Fortunately, he was blessed with young priests who had the zest and imagination to help keep the outer and the inner man all of a piece.

This was difficult because each year the poor of Korea endure a period called "spring suffering." The *kimchi* pots outside the mud huts are empty, the rice has been eaten, and now they search the hills for herbs and grasses, for anything edible, until the crops come again. At the end of the Korean war "the spring suffering" extended to all seasons. People on the run don't plant and harvest. If something was planted it was often harvested by Communist guerrillas who lived off the land. On top of it all a drought caused one bad growing season. Famine became a way of life.

While Harold Henry was getting various agencies to supply food, some of his young priests were planning ways to keep the people fed through all seasons. For example, Father John Russell took a good hard look at the situation and let his imagination take wing.

He saw that the Yellow Sea was rich in fish—mackerel, shark, abalone, oysters. The Yellow Sea, though, is so fierce it has defied the islanders through the centuries. It has one of the fastest and highest tides in the world, and contrary winds against a high fast tide cause heavy seas. This, in addition to typhoons and dense fogs, makes fishing a hazard. A missionary said: "A

fisherman told me that every time he went out he vomited. Not seasick-
ness. Fear. Imagine living that way year after year."

The trouble, Father Russell decided, was not so much with the sea as
with the structure of the boats. He told Harold Henry: "They are small,
poorly powered and flat-bottomed. They are built for a fine day. To build
for a storm, more design, more keel, and more power are needed."

As a beginning, a shipyard was built, Harold Henry approved the project
and the Society of Saint Columban raised the money.

Father Russell found a boat "fanatic" in the United States Eighth Army
by the name of Colonel Robert J. Kriwanek. The colonel preached the
shocking doctrine, "Build boats out of concrete."

Most people, especially the fishermen, gave a sceptical laugh at the mention of ferro-concrete boats. In the middle of the laughter Father Russell
asked Cyril Chisholm, naval architect to the Irish Sea Fisheries Board, to
design a seventy-foot motor vessel out of concrete.

Nothing in the history of that part of Korea caused so much excitement
as the boat's maiden voyage. There it was—floating! A ferro-concrete
boat that will not rust, scale or deteriorate in salt water. A boat that is
fireproof and one that rot and worms will not touch. Here was a cheaper,
safer and lighter boat than any of the fishermen had ever dreamed of own-
ing.

The archbishop took me to Hallim, a few miles west of Cheju city, so
that I might see other imaginative ways young Columbans were helping
people help themselves. Out there the land is dark and brooding, reminis-
cent of the American West at its most desolate. Father Patrick McGlinchey
was attracted to such land because it reminded him of the west of Ireland
and also because he could buy it for less than two dollars an acre. The Koreans considered it useless, and that was an advantage because then the missionary could prove to them that they might make better use of the very
land of which they despaired.

He divided 1,200 acres into farms of 25 acres each. The recipient of a
farm had ten years to pay for it; the money repaid went into a revolving
fund that would eventually establish 500 farms. The young priest gave
away seed and grain and a few pigs of purebred stock, Durocs and Chester
Whites until, in time, the farmers were raising 15,000 pigs a year. He
taught them how to help chickens survive the drafty climate, beginning
with 200 purebred Leghorns and New Hampshires.

The value of putting lime on the land was something the Columban had
to prove by demonstration. When he came to Hallim he used to ask, "Why

don't you put lime on your land?" and was told that the farmers saw no need for it and besides there was none to be had.

"I pointed out," said Father McGlinchey, "that the coast abounds in sea-shells and these shells, if crushed into powder, make good lime. People grinned, said it was interesting, but did not believe a word of it.

"I got our 4-H boys to draw shells from the shore, crush them into powder and dress their plots with it. I offered a prize of a thoroughbred hog to the boy who produced the biggest crop of barley on his newly limed plot, and a second prize of a crossbred hog to the boy with the next best crop. The boy who won the first prize reaped twice the amount of barley as yielded by plots of the same size that lacked lime."

To start another of his many self-help projects, Father McGlinchey installed a series of hotbeds, producing 10,000 plants, mainly cabbage and tomatoes, for distribution among 4-H members. The youngsters were required to cultivate according to instructions. After the crops matured the 4-H members were asked to pay back twice the original amount received for distribution among other members. The Columbans helped them market in groups rather than singly to get a better price.

Since Father McGlinchey is from County Donegal it was inevitable that he think of sheep and weaving when casting about for other ways to help his parishioners help themselves. Again he was confronted by skeptics—the land around Hallim makes for poor pastures, and besides the Japanese had tried to raise sheep there and had failed.

Still the missionary went ahead and imported a few Corriedale sheep from Japan and distributed them to farmers willing to take a chance on hand-feeding them and grazing them on the rough local grasses. At the same time he sent a girl from his parish to Cheju City to learn to cord and spin yarn. The first yarn was made into sweaters knitted in imitation of those made on the Aran Islands off the west coast of Ireland.

The most important step in this handweaving industry was the arrival of Columban Sisters from Ireland in 1962. They came to run the factory and to look after the ever-growing number of girls who worked there. In factories and handcraft schools in Ireland the Sisters had learned the art of weaving the delicate patterns and bright color combinations found in Irish tweed. Kim Samuel, an artist, mastered the secret of the dyer's art that the Sisters had learned from experts in Dublin, Artane, Avoca and Foxford. Another artist, Athanasius Im, a former catechist, was hired as a designer.

The success of the textile plants gave new impetus to sheep-breeding on the island. By the time I was there, in 1975, there were 1,300 sheep on the main farm. The Koreans had to learn to shear sheep; instead of shearing away the wool in one piece, they snipped it off in lumps making processing difficult. Father McGlinchey imported a dozen pairs of hand shears from Japan and Father Peter Tierney from the Korean mainland. Father Tierney taught the Koreans the art of shearing as he had learned it on his father's farm in Galway.

I was so impressed with what I saw at the weaving factory that I bombarded the Sisters with questions. Sales are so good, they said, that eighty girls are employed at the factory making blankets, wall hangings, fringed rungs and tartan skirts; and approximately 300 women and girls work at home knitting sweaters, vests, coats, dresses, scarves, caps, mittens, afghans and ponchos, all of 100 percent wool.

The things they made were so sophisticated that they were much in demand in Seoul. Miss Korea helped popularize Hallim tweed by including it in her wardrobe when she set out for the United States.

Father McGlinchey brought cattle to Hallim with the same dramatic flair he did everything else. He needed 450 head and somehow found the money for them, but learned it was poor economy to ship less than 1,000 head over the 5,000-mile route from Australia to Korea. What to do about the 550 cattle the farm could not afford? McGlinchey interested Korean Airlines in taking 300 head for its farm on Cheju. But what about the remaining 250? The missionary flew to Australia and, after long negotiation, got the company to agree to sell him 250 more on credit. He found Archbishop Henry willing to send a message to Columban world headquarters in Killiney asking for a guarantee for the loan.

Then came the problem of how to get the cattle ashore. The huge freighter would have to drop anchor far out in deep water. The plan had been to have the cattle arrive in summer and swim ashore, but all the dickering had delayed the project so that the cattle arrived in December, a month of dangerous, choppy water.

Father McGlinchey turned to the United States Army for barges and tugboats. It turned out to be an armada silhouetted on the horizon—the huge freighter carrying 1,000 purebred Australian cattle, flanked by barges and tugboats. The people of Cheju were so excited they kept yelling, "The cattle are coming! The cattle are coming!"—a cry that echoed across the hills.

Father McGlinchey was the calmest man in the crowd. He kept looking around wondering if he had forgotten anything. The logistics of moving 1,000 head of cattle safely ashore and then trailing them twelve miles across the hills to a 2,000-acre ranch were frightening. It had meant transforming the wharf of a Korean fishing village into a huge temporary stockyard. Corrals were built, hay and grain provided, and temporary water and power lines set up.

Father McGlinchey saw the barges move into position to load the reluctant cattle. "God has blessed us again," he said. "Look at the tranquil water —hardly a ripple. You seldom see that in December."

By the time I reached Hallim, Father McGlinchey could look back over twenty years of achievement. He recalled how he used to lean on a black stone wall, the kind that surrounds each tiny field in Cheju, and watch farmers do things the hard way. He was amused and saddened at the way they used wild ponies during planting season. When the seeds were scattered over the field, the farmer and his wife and children would chase a herd of ponies around and around, chanting a haunting song, until the seeds were covered and the ground smooth and packed.

"When you see a man scratching the surface of the land with an ox-drawn wooden plough, the first inclination is to laugh," said the missionary, "but then you see the beads of sweat as he pushes and wrestles the plough behind the unwilling animal. You feel sympathy and anger."

"I decided come hell or high water I would show the people here a better way. Oxfam gave the money to buy the first tractor, plough and disc harrow ever seen on Cheju."

The first driver, unknown to Father McGlinchey, was an epileptic. He turned over the tractor and nearly killed himself. As the missionary rushed the boy to a makeshift clinic in Hallim, he vowed he would see to it that Hallim would soon have a first-rate clinic.

By the time I made my tour of Hallim, there were twenty-five tractors in the farm equipment pool, and Hallim had a first-rate clinic. The three Columban Sisters who operated it said that they were assisted by a staff of nineteen, which included two doctors and two registered nurses. About 1,000 patients came each month, they said.

Archbishop Henry and Father McGlinchey were kindred souls; both had a "no-sweat" attitude toward life. Both had unbounded energy, freewheeling ideas and an impatience with the slowness of the way things moved.

While he looked over the farm in Hallim the archbishop said, "Father McGlinchey has twenty-two ideas in one day. My task is to hold him down to two a month. When he has $10,000 promised for cattle next month he wants to spend it this month. Once an idea is decided on though, I allow him to follow it without interference. He likes that. I learned in the army that you give a man an assignment but don't tell him how to carry it out."

Although there was occasional friction between those two powerful personalities, both agreed that no one should confine his aspirations only to worldly matters, because there could not really be a kingdom of heaven on earth. Material advantages seem like the trappings of paradise until boredom sets in. Something spiritual is needed or life gets out of balance.

To help keep balance in Cheju's social and economic betterment, Archbishop Henry did something dramatic. He brought from the United States a contemplative order of nuns to establish a monastery on the farmland in Hallim. It was in Minneapolis that he approached a foundation of the Sisters of St. Clare, usually called the Poor Clares, to ask if they would be willing to come to Korea.

He and I jolted across a rocky, rutted road to the monastery that stands alone in the middle of vast, windswept acreage. He explained to me that the Sisters are not to engage in an "active" apostolate. "I did not ask the Sisters of St. Clare to come to Korea for catechetical purposes. They are to sacrifice themselves each day in lives of sacrifice and prayer. Rather than tell people about God they are to tell God about these people."

My journal, for Sunday, January 26, 1975, reminds me of how bitterly cold it was in the monastery chapel when Archbishop Henry said Mass. The chill was so numbing in the refectory that the nuns suggested I wear my parka at lunch.

We talked mainly about the small farm the Sisters operate to keep body and soul together. The land they work is volcanic in origin. For centuries Mount Halla, an extinct volcano, spewed lava which cooled to form the porous basalt that dominates. The weather contributes to the difficulty of farming, for Cheju is situated at the center of a crossroads of the winds. Cold Siberian winds blow down from the north, pick up momentum across the open Yellow Sea, meet Mount Halla and are deflected to the eastern and western side of the island. Someone called it "a well-ventilated island" and one Sister said that Chejuites are such loud talkers because they grow up shouting down the wind.

Toward the end of lunch one of the nuns observed that I am a light eater.

"I just prefer it that way," I said. "It has nothing to do with sacrifice."

"When the right act is preferred and not done as a conscious effort, that is virtue at its best," she said, and added, "I read that somewhere."

After returning to the archbiship's residence in Cheju City, I told a Columban of how impressed I had been with the Poor Clares. He said: "The wisdom of the archbishop's decision is already evident. Attendance at Mass is greatly increased. The children, though not instructed directly by the nuns, have a great awareness of them. And their appetite for religious doctrine classes has grown. The leaven is working."

·9·

Walking Old Paths

When I visited Archbishop Henry he had lived in semiretirement on Cheju Island for nearly four years. Most of his forty-two years as a missionary had been spent on the mainland in and around Mokpo and Kwangju.

To retrace the steps of his ministry we planned to fly to the mainland. Again the weather turned vicious. After twenty-four hours the blizzard paused long enough for our flight to Kwangju. At the airport, Sister Enda, a medical doctor from County Mayo, was waiting to take us by ambulance the fifty-six miles across mountains to a hospital operated by Columban Sisters in Mokpo.

The blizzard returned with renewed fury as we stepped from the airport terminal. Police stopped us at the foot of the mountain ordering us to join busses and cars at the edge of the road waiting out the storm. They did not reckon with the likes of Archbishop Henry and Sister Enda, both determined to push on, and so we did. Part way up the mountain a military blockade confronted us. When the young lieutenant said that we must wait until visibility returned to something near normal, arguments flew back and forth. The lieutenant, slamming the door with annoyance, said, "Try it!"

Our ambulance driver must have known the mountain road by heart for he could not see any part of it. Fortunately, zero visibility kept me from seeing the narrowness of the road, the steepness of the ravines and the lack of guardrails; I felt confident that we would not meet another vehicle coming toward us, for no one on the other side of the mountain had the spirit and determination of the archbishop and the nun in our ambulance.

After midnight we arrived at the hospital in Mokpo. Sister Enda took my blood pressure: a resounding 160/110.

The next day, in trying to lower the blood pressure, she had me stay in bed. For several hours she sat in my room answering questions about the hospital, how it started and how it grew.

Twenty years earlier Harold Henry had begged the Columban Sisters to come to Korea to start a hospital. When Sister Enda and three other nuns arrived they found that their new home was a mud hut, with mud floor, composed of four tiny rooms. Olive drab army blankets covered four army cots, and another blanket hung across the window to impede somewhat the penetrating wind coming in off the sea that January night in 1955. For light, they had a candle stuck into a nail that had been driven through a jagged block of wood.

The work of the Columban Sisters in Mokpo was blessed from the start. Their story is filled with examples of what some people would call serendipity and others the grace of Providence. From a four-room mud hut had grown a modern hospital.

The day the Columban Sisters opened their makeshift clinic thirty-seven patients arrived. Each morning thereafter the numbers grew. The Koreans began to line up at the door at four in the morning. Even though the rain might be beating down and a cold wind coming in off the Yellow Sea, the sick stood there patiently accepting the misery of it all. Some had come as far as seventy miles and some from the hundreds of islands that dot the sea on the southwest coast.

"Often they went to their villages in the hills," said Sister Enda, "and told friends and neighbors about the strange foreign ladies in white who wore crucifixes and talked bad Korean with a strange accent. The more they talked the larger the crowds grew. The Sisters attended to patients all morning and afternoon and in the evening made house calls. Each day it became more evident that with more than a million people in the area, we would need more floor space, equipment and helping hands."

The Sisters managed to build a two-story clinic that turned out to be too small the day it was finished. The patients kept coming, most on foot, but some on the backs of their friends. A common sight was a wife with her husband on her back, arriving after an exhausting journey over the hills in the burning heat.

Harold Henry was behind the Sisters helping them every inch of the way. As Sister Enda recalled, "He would give you anything. He kept nothing for himself. And when he gave you something there were no strings attached. When he gives something he gives it. So I was always careful not to ask for too much."

When he saw the new clinic was too cramped, Henry offered his own house to the Sisters to turn into operating rooms and wards. Sister Enda felt embarrassed at putting him out of his own home, but he said, "No sweat." He would build a place in Kwangju and move there, and so he did. He assured her the move made sense because Kwangju was more centrally located and his priests could reach him more readily.

The archbishop and I went by train from Mokpo to Kwangju. In passing through Naju he spoke with a certain poignancy of how lonely he had been there forty years earlier.

He recalled how he had walked the muddy streets, passing between rows of small Korean shops and an occasional larger Japanese store, all the while running the gauntlet of curious eyes. White-robed, stately Korean men in black stove-pipe hats stared at him. Women, in their easy-fitting skirts and trousers, seemed in a hurry; with so much to do, they paid scant attention to a stranger. Groups of children followed him, keeping a safe distance and turning attention to something else when he returned their gaze. How alone he had felt!

In Kwangju the archbishop took me to the seminary and retreat center dedicated in 1962. As our car climbed a steep hill I was startled by the architecture of a building poised at the crest: It was a reproduction of Moreau Seminary on the campus at the University of Notre Dame. The architect in Korea probably researched newly built seminaries in the United States and found the Moreau blueprints. The seminary was crowded with 291 students and 16 faculty members.

The archbishop said that he believed his heart attack came from the pressures he felt raising money in the United States for the seminary. Then I understood his mood of a week earlier when he had come to my room one evening in Cheju looking much older than his sixty-five years. "I am drained tonight," he said. "All day I have been meeting with Korean clergy who want to relocate the seminary. I'll fight that all the way to Rome, if I must."

All over Kwangju were evidences of Harold Henry's vitality—clinics, schools, churches, all kinds of things for body and soul. Revisiting these places seem to rejuvenate him the way our morning sessions used to back in Cheju.

Out of courtesy the archbishop insisted on flying with me to Seoul to see me off to the United States. We checked into Columban House and I walked around Seoul discovering what a lovely city it is. I had expected drabness. And the people have so much style! It is the way Paris used to look.

At the airport Harold Henry made arrangements with the manager of an airline so that I would have a better seat than was called for on the ticket. He was an expert at such. Fortunately, I was seated near the front because tough little Korean baggage handlers carried a dozen Korean babies to the back of the plane. At that point missionaries and Peace Corps volunteers took over; they would receive free transportation for delivering the children to couples who would adopt them in the States. A few of the children were far enough beyond infancy to be pesky. A nun told me about one little girl who had stuffed her sister's clothes into the toilet. A stewardess turned one of the plane's curtains into a makeshift something to cover the undressed child.

It was a long, trying flight. Returning from the Far East means flying eastward, and that always brings jet lag at its worst. There were no long delays, though; the longest was waiting for baggage in the South Bend airport: forty minutes.

·10·

The Last Days

A phone call came from Archbishop Henry early in August 1975; he was in Iowa to attend a wedding. I said that I wished he would go through the manuscript word for word and that Killiney would be the best place to do this because in the archives we might find the answers to some questions. I offered to pay his way to Ireland where we could spend two weeks putting the final touches to *Light in the Far East*.

When we met at O'Hare, on August 4, I regretted having suggested the trip. He approached across the lobby of the International Building as though each step were a painful effort and might well be his last. I remembered the oxygen tank that a Korean gardener used to carry to his room to help him through the night, but now the tank was far away and a purple tinge was on his face, especially on the lips.

The archbishop always knew the best place to wait for a plane in any airport, and so he led me to a VIP room operated by Aer Lingus, a replica of an old-fashioned drawing room with crystal chandeliers and antique furniture. Of course he knew the manager of Aer Lingus in Chicago, a Mr. Conway.

"I want to get off when we stop at Montreal to make a phone call to a Korean bartender who used to teach for me in Kwangju," he said.

"No one is allowed off the plane at Montreal," the manager said. "We are on the ground for only a brief time. We board passengers, but no one gets off."

There was a challenge!

Later two stewardesses told Harold Henry the same thing. Each time he became more determined. Of course he did get off at Montreal and made the phone call to the Korean bartender who used to teach in Kwangju, but the phone just rang and rang and nobody answered.

That night's trip across the Atlantic was a dark one. The archbishop insisted that I sit next to the window and he took the uneasy middle seat. A man and two girls behind us were compulsive talkers. From the things they said we judged they were members of the IRA visiting Canada to raise funds. They were a tough trio and sounded meanspirited.

In Killiney we carefully checked the manuscript. Several Columbans who had spent years in Korea also went through it. The typical reaction was expressed in a note that Father Bernard Smyth attached to the manuscript: "I have thoroughly enjoyed reading this. It is a story that moves quickly, easily and (for me at any rate) is engrossing."

On August 17 I celebrated what the Koreans call my *hwankap*. When a man has lived sixty years he has completed one cycle of the lunar calendar. By now he should have accomplished all of his ambitions, say the Koreans, and should be free to spend his remaining years seeking serenity. This time of transition is marked by a solemn ceremony, the *hwankap*.

By way of celebration the archbishop, Father Smyth, Ruth Brennan and I dined at the Glen of the Downs, a country restaurant that overlooks the Wicklow Hills. Its simplicity was a contrast to Archbishop Henry's *hwankap* in 1969, the largest birthday celebration ever held in southwestern Korea. More than 5,000 Korean Catholics came to it; some 200 priests attended, along with 17 bishops, Stephen Cardinal Kim, Korea's first cardinal, the Archbishop Ippolito Rotoli, papal delegate to Korea.

A few nights later I had a second *hwankap* when the president of Ireland invited the archbishop and me to dine with him and his wife. I had come to know Cearbhall O'Dalaigh on my first trip to Ireland (he was chief justice then) and saw much of him on succeeding trips.

He was always arranging interesting interviews for me, with Cardinal Conway, Eamon DeValera and others, and this night he would try to arrange something else for me. Two *gardai* in a high-powered car came for us in Killiney and took us to the president's home; later we went on to dine at Hunter's Hotel in Rathnew, County Wicklow.

President O'Dalaigh wanted to introduce me to the owner; the hotel had been in her family for 200 years. Thackeray had come there to write and so had Sir Walter Scott. The present owner wanted a history of the hotel written. Cearbhall O'Dalaigh suggested that I live there while writing the history.

It was the kind of opportunity that sounds good to the ear but did not reach the heart. Unless I feel an inner push to go ahead and do it, the work is not for me.

President O'Dalaigh expected that he might receive a phone call during dinner announcing the death of DeValera. That afternoon he had visited the former president of Ireland in a Dublin nursing home.

"How do you feel, Dev?" he asked.

The answer was a slow, labored, "I am . . . not in . . . good form."

The next day Archbishop Henry and Father Richard Steinhilber, the superior general of the Columbans, asked if I would also write the biography of Archbishop Patrick Cronin, a Columban in the Philippines. I agreed to do that but said that I would not be free to leave for the Philippines until the following fall.

At Notre Dame I had been saying for two years that I intended to take an early retirement to give full time to writing. So now on the Aer Lingus flight home I drafted a letter of resignation; the academic year about to begin would be my last.

In the letter I said that the principal reason for leaving teaching, one awkward to speak of and almost impossible to explain, had to do with the way I have made all major decisions: Minor decisions I make out of my head, but major ones come from the intuitions. They have to "feel right" and this one feels right.

Were I working for a business or industry I may not have said it just that way out of fear of sounding foolish. But surely Notre Dame would understand, and did. I agreed to continue teaching in the graduate program in summers but as September of 1976 would be retired. The university was generous in offering me office space and secretarial help for life.

At O'Hare the archbishop was waiting for me, as he said he would be, in the Skylounge. He had left Ireland the day before to go to Boston and on to Montreal to visit some Koreans, including the Korean bartender who used to teach in Kwangju.

During dinner we agreed to meet a week later in Minneapolis. The Minnesotan who, a year and a half earlier, had told me anecdotes at breakfast about an archbishop in Korea was having a twenty-fifth wedding anniversary. Yes, we would be there to help him and his wife celebrate.

In Minneapolis the archbishop took me to Saint Mary's Hospital where he had spent three months following his heart attack. What a reception he received! Word ran along the corridors that Archbishop Henry was visitng and nurses, orderlies, nun and doctors came hurrying toward us. There was suddenly a gala atmosphere all through the hospital.

I talked with doctors who had cared for the archbishop at the time of the attack. They said that anyone with such a damaged heart just shouldn't be alive, not according to medical science.

As said earlier, the stress of raising funds for the major seminary may have been responsible for the decline in the archbishop's health. Perhaps his illness was foreshadowed in a letter sent from Rome as far back as November of 1963: "This council is growing very tiring. My brain is about petrified now, and I believe I would vote for anything just to get away."

The attack came on Christmas Day, 1963, in Minneapolis. He felt chest pain that morning but ignored it because he wanted to keep a promise. He had promised Mary Zepp, a woman in her eighties, that he would drive her from Minneapolis to Alma to have Christmas dinner with her brother; he felt a special obligation to her because she had built St. Philip's Church in Kwangju in memory of her father. He kept the promise and drove her a hundred miles over icy roads.

On the way home the chest pains kept recurring. When he reached Annunciation Church at ten o'clock a young priest insisted on sending for an ambulance. Harold Henry spent the next six weeks in an oxygen tent in the intensive care unit at St. Mary's Hospital. It pleased him the way Sister Josepha pulled no punches in dealing with him.

He said to her, "When I go will I be doubled up in pain and gasping for breath the way they do in the movies?"

"No," she answered. "You'll probably go so fast the nurse on duty won't even know it right away."

As we left the hospital the archbishop recalled with feeling the days of his confinement. "The restrictions were many," he said. "Don't get excited. Don't climb stairs. I had the reputation of being an active fellow and so they put me on phenobarbital. That turned me into a zombie. I fail to see how anyone can get a 'kick' out of that stuff. I begged the doctor to take me off it. He did after I promised that I would follow instructions."

The archbishop insisted on going to the Minneapolis airport with my wife and me to see us off. In the coffee shop I led him into recalling the changes he had seen in Korea since his arrival there in 1933. That was something he enjoyed doing. He recalled with satisfaction that there had been fewer than a hundred thousand Catholics there on his arrival, but now, in September of 1975, there were over a million.

"In those early days," he said, "there were few Koreans among the clergy. Now thirteen of the seventeen bishops in South Korea are of native birth. Of the 900 priests and 2,800 sisters and 180 brothers a majority are Korean. That will increase. There are about 600 young men preparing for the priesthood in the two major seminaries." (By 1985 that number had grow to 775 with from 50 to 70 applications turned away each year for lack of space.)

Harold Henry had also seen great changes in the Columban Foreign Mission Society. He had watched it grow from a handful of priests to nearly one thousand. Its work, focused at first in China, had spread to include Ireland, Great Britain, the United States, Australia, New Zealand, Korea, Burma, Taiwan, Japan, Fiji, Peru, Chile and the Philippines.

When the call came for our flight, I remember thinking that surely this is the last time the archbishop and I will meet. He must have been thinking that, too.

I felt so sure that he would be dead before the book was published that I wrote the final paragraph in such a way that when I received news of his death I could add to it without any transition.

So I wrote that the biggest change Harold Henry found late in life was an increased awareness of mystery. He had said that reexamining his life for his biography had been the greatest spiritual retreat he had ever made; it made him see how ordinary men do extraordinary things. How God writes straight with crooked lines. He saw the work of the Columbans as a conspiracy between God and man to get something done. He was glad he had been given a role to play in the mystery. He could think of no other life he would rather have lived.

Death came to Archbishop Harold Henry at prayer on the morning of Monday March 1, 1976, at age sixty-six. Upon receiving the word I called the publisher in New York asking that the manuscript be returned so that I might change some of the verb tenses from present to past. Meanwhile I made arrangements for Father Joseph Crofts, who lived at the archbishop's residence, to send details of the funeral.

The archbishop was in his tiny chapel, one built by his Minnesota friends, when the end came suddenly. Had he been given a choice of where and how to die, this would have been the place and manner of his choosing. Such a death was strangely calm for a man who had feared execution at the hands of the Japanese, had shown heroism in Patton's attack in Germany, had outwitted guerrilla fighters in Korea—and had survived mishaps in the air, typhoons at sea and blizzards in the mountains.

His dog barking at the chapel door attracted the attention of the housekeeper. She found the archbishop slumped forward on the prie-dieu in front of the altar.

The word spread rapidly, and from early morning there was a continuous flow of mourners who came to say prayers for the dead. Everyone was free to come quickly because March 1 was Revolutionary Day, a state holiday. As one Korean said: "He was considerate even in his dying."

Several thousand people stood in the schoolyard where the Mass was concelebrated by more than a hundred priests on the bright sunny afternoon. Cardinal Kim told of some of the things Harold Henry had done for the needy and the lepers: "His life was his sermon. The way he lived was a message to all of us to live a life immersed in love for our fellow-man." The mourners, from all over the island and the mainland, represented all walks of life. The president of Korea had sent a representative and a floral arrangement.

The funeral cortege began moving toward the east up a hill near the edge of town. It was led by a band and followed by a group of nurses and hundreds of students. Then came the hearse; it was actually an ambulance that the Columban Sisters had covered with white flowers before bringing it from their clinic in Hallim. Behind it walked the cardinal, the apostolic nuncio, the bishops and priests.

Then came the mourners. By their very numbers they proved that Harold Henry had achieved the *adaptation totale* that the French missionary had recommended to him forty-two years earlier. The procession of 15,000 Koreans, so vast that it brought all traffic to a standstill, stretched for more than a mile with men and women walking six abreast. They proceeded up the hill reciting the rosary and singing hymns all the way to the cemetery three miles outside the city. Again Harold Henry became a pioneer, for he was the first religious to be buried inside those grounds.

When it was over Father Crofts wrote: "They buried him as if he were a king, with a mound of earth higher and bigger than the rest. And with a large area in front for people to gather. Everybody cooperated to make it a fitting tribute to his excellency's forty-two years in Korea. That's because all who met him loved him. All of those honors were given to him not because he was a Catholic archbishop, but because he was himself."

·11·

Mindanao Mission

The next book was to be a biography of Archbishop Patrick Cronin, a Columban missionary stationed in the Philippines. To begin research I returned, in 1976, to the archives of the Columban Fathers in Ireland.

That summer I lived in the room Archbishop Harold Henry had occupied when we were in Killiney a year earlier. It was a delightful room with high ceiling, attractive fireplace, flowered carpet and bay window framed with a proscenium arch. Working there at a walnut desk I looked out on Killiney Bay and Bray Head, a view forever changing depending on weather and time of day.

Leafing through pages of the Columban magazine, *The Far East*, was like listening to a sermon on mortality. For instance, I might begin in the morning with a page of fresh young faces, newly ordained priests, followed by a list of their assignments—China, Korea, the Philippines. Within an hour I would come upon photographs of those young pastors working with their people in fishing villages, banana groves or leper colonies. In the afternoon they showed signs of middle age—waistline thickened, face broadened, muscles beginning to sag. Then quite suddenly a photograph edged in black. A brief biography. A request that you pray for the repose of a soul.

Often I was distracted by something in *The Far East* that had nothing to do with the research at hand. For instance, I came upon the Chinese proverb: "Desire and passions need not injure the heart, but self-righteousness eats it like a cancer."

This brought to mind a man on Aer Lingus who boomed through the night sentence after sentence of self-righteousness. He assured the stewardess several times that he never touched coffee or tea, and bragged to the man across the aisle that alcohol had never crossed his lips.

"I'm making this trip because I can afford it," he proclaimed to all of us.

"My brother can't afford it. Alcohol. Mother used to warn him against that stuff."

Through the night, above the Atlantic, I wondered what that incessant speaker looked like. In the morning I saw a most depraved face. Self-righteousness may have destroyed his face as much as alcohol destroyed his brother's.

I found mealtime in Killiney most entertaining. The five priests on the superior general's council had traveled widely enough to know such details as the best flight from Cagayan de Oro to Ozamis, and visiting missionaries spoke of places I had not heard of but would, through the years, come to know—Chiba City, Lambasa, Kumamoto.

Their conversation was seasoned with humor. One Columban told of an old Irish priest who was walking with two fellow priests in Dublin. Somehow or other he became separated from them. So he stopped a policeman and said, "Did you see two fellows walking by here without me?"

Another Columban told of the man from County Kerry who left for a honeymoon in Dublin without his bride. "Why didn't you bring your wife?" someone asked. "Ah, she has already been to Dublin," the groom said.

Irish expressions were bandied about the table. One that I recall: "He's out of the same stable!"

While talking with the Columbans I began to realize that telling Archbishop Cronin's life story would be more difficult than telling Archbishop Henry's. Harold Henry was most willing to have his biography written, but Patrick Cronin was not. He consented to the ordeal only because the superior general had said that it would be a good thing for Saint Columban's Foreign Mission Society.

One missionary who had spent a lot of time with Patrick Cronin said that he had never heard the archbishop mention that his father had been executed by the Irish Republican Army. So when Father Bernard Smyth drove me to Moneygall, where Patrick Cronin had been born, we decided to search out an old IRA gunman who might know the story.

We rode through a gentle valley that separates the Sieve Bloom Mountains. It is dairy country with rolling hills and twisting lanes held close by hedges and stone walls.

"This country," said Father Smyth, "bears little resemblance to the place where Pat Cronin has spent most of his life." He said that I would find in Mindanao spiny mountains, dense jungle with dark, sluggish rivers crowded to the very edge by tropical growth.

We got lost in country lanes and stopped several times to ask directions at cottages before finding Andy Cody. At seventy-seven he was remarkably lively and moved with the springiness of a well-trained athlete.

We learned that when Patrick Cronin was three years old, his father, Sergeant Henry Cronin, of the Royal Irish Constabulary, had moved his family from Moneygall to Tullamore. It was during the time of The Troubles, or as Andy Cody called it, "the war among brothers."

Sergeant Cronin became a victim of those cheerless times on Halloween of 1920. As he left his home to start back to the barracks, a few hundred yards away, he was felled by bullets just outside the front door.

Andy said that Father Cosgrove knew all about the dark days, and so he led us through narrow lanes to visit the pastor of Dunkerrin. The old man with haunted eyes, quavering hands and tremulous voice said that he recalled nothing about Sergeant Cronin's death but remembered something similar happened at Toomivara on the night of Saint Patrick's Feast in 1918.

The IRA had decided to shoot two members of the Royal Irish Constabulary as a protest against something long forgotten. They knew that two sergeants always attended evening services at the church in Toomivara, and it was there they shot down Sergeant Rock and Sergeant Scanlon. "To this day they are sorry for having shot Rock," said the old pastor, "he was such a fine man." In the chilly rectory the ancient priest forgot some of his pain as he shook with the excitement of reliving the past. He repeated again and again, "The spirit of revenge was abroad in the land!"

We continued on to Moneygall to visit Rosanna Fleming, who in her eighties clearly recalled the day Patrick Cronin was baptized. She still lived across the street from the church where she had held the child above the black stone baptismal font on the very day of his birth, November 30, 1913. The ceremony was held that day not because the child was sickly but because the priest would not return to Moneygall for a week or more.

Since her godson had eventually sailed for the Philippines, she followed closely every scrap of news from there, especially from the island of Mindanao. Through the years she heard about earthquakes, tidal waves, ambushes by Moros, murdered missionaries, American guerrilla fighters and Japanese attacks. All of which helped her conclude that Mindanao was no place for the fainthearted.

In speaking of how Sergeant Cronin had been gunned down in Tulamore, Miss Fleming sighed, "'Twas a sad time. 'Twas a bad time.'"

Father Smyth and I drove on to Tullamore where Patrick had grown into boyhood. There we found his sister, Peggy, living in the old family home on Henry Street. She said that when her mother, Mary Murphy Cronin, was widowed she had the burden of rearing four children, Margaret, Kathleen, James and Patrick, the youngest not quite seven.

Since Bernard Smyth had been in the seminary with Patrick Cronin, he and Peggy spent much of the evening recalling those days.

"He was excited about everything he was involved in," said Father Smyth. "He got into whatever he was doing completely."

When Patrick Cronin was ordained, December 21, 1937, the Columbans were working in China, Korea, Burma and the Philippines. Of these countries he had no particular favorite, and it was just as well because no one asked him to make a choice.

The young priests continued to study for a few months after ordination, until one day in the spring of 1938 appointments were posted on the bulletin board. Father Cronin and eight of his classmates were assigned to the Philippines. They would be the first Columbans to work in Mindanao.

Mindanao!

During seminary days Patrick Cronin had read articles in *The Far East* about Luzon, the island at the top of the archipelago. The only thing he knew about Mindanao was that it was at the bottom. The rest of the world knew even less. Yet within five years the name of Mindanao would be much repeated during newscasts on radio.

·12·

Walks in the Evening

Archbishop Patrick Cronin often told his young priests, "Say your prayers and take a stroll every evening." He and I strolled each evening around and around the circular park in front of the *convento* in Cagayan de Oro while he spoke of his early days in the Philippines.

How fast the years had gone! He recalled the early Sunday morning, December 11, 1938, when from the deck of the inter-island boat, the *Panay*, he had his first look at Mindanao. Bishop James T. Hayes, S.J., had come up from Cagayan to welcome the young missionaries and explain that he would transfer the province gradually from the administration of the Jesuits to the Columbans so that the transition would be easy for all concerned.

The newly arrived Columbans learned that while English and Spanish and Tagalog are most used, still there are at least sixty dialects spoken in the islands. Tagalog, considered the national language, is confined mainly to the Manila area and its surrounding provinces on the island of Luzon. Down in Mindanao they would need Visayan, a dialect difficult for them because it has no similarity with languages of the West.

Father Cronin was sent to live with a Filipino priest who placed him under the tutelage of an old man "more interested in learning English than in teaching me Visayan." From the old man came a smattering of linguistic information that did not add up to much. Father Cronin learned, for example, that the passive voice is stronger than the active voice, just the opposite from English. It is more forceful to say, "You are thanked by me," than "I thank you." Knowing such a nicety had little value when words and grammar were needed.

During our first evening walk, the archbishop said that one of the most pleasant years of his life was the one he spent learning the ropes with two classmates, Fathers Francis Chapman and William Hennessey. Father Chapman was appointed as pastor and the other two became his assistants in Tangub.

Father Cronin arrived in Tangub to find the church plaza, the heart of every Filipino town, about a half-mile from Panguil Bay where fishermen lived and where hundreds of *bancas* were anchored to the shore. As he and Father Chapman walked a quarter-mile between two rows of nipa palm huts, he felt he was living inside one of the photographs in a mission magazine. There was something picturesque about the way the houses were placed under the shade of coconut trees against a dense background of banana plants.

The two Columbans came upon the church in the center of the plaza, an imposing structure devoid of architectural design and style. The only definite feature was a concrete floor. It wasn't too bad, though, they told each other. Not considering that for nearly forty years—following the expulsion of Spanish friars in 1898—Tangub had been without a resident priest. Once or twice a year an old Spanish padre had visited there. When he died in 1932 his parishioners built a church and called it San Miguel in his honor.

Father Chapman pointed above the main altar to an imposing statue of San Miguel with sword held high. Neither Columban could foresee that within less than five years the sword would disappear, stolen by Japanese soldiers, and that the church would be destroyed by Japanese bombs.

Father Chapman said to his assistants that Bishop Hayes had told him that there were nearly fifty village chapels scattered over a parish stretching twenty-five miles along the seaside and extending deep into mountains dense with jungle. There were supposed to be about 41,000 parishioners.

The three priests developed a plan known as "doing the *barrios*." They said Mass in the larger *barrios* once a month and in the smaller ones every three months.

On a typical visit Father Cronin came riding into the *barrio* early in the evening astride a horse he now felt at home with. He visited the sick in the locality before giving instructions to the children and hearing confessions. The following morning he again heard confessions and then officiated at marriages, said Mass and administered baptism.

Before riding back to Tangub he spent some time chatting with the people, hoping his Visayan was improving. The parisioners were hospitable to the point of embarrassing the young priest with their kindness. For example, in most houses there is but one bed—Filipinos usually sleep on the floor—and this was reserved for the padre.

The agreeable arrangement of the three young priests working together, in what seemed high adventure, came to an end May 1, 1940. On that day Bishop Hayes took away 18,000 parishioners from Tangub to establish a parish ten miles down the road. He appointed Patrick Cronin as the first pastor in Bonifacio.

The first problem was to build a church in Bonifacio. The archbishop told me that he should have started by building a house for himself. Instead, he rented a place with a galvanized roof and the heat was unbearable. Next he rented a place in which a farmer stored grain and that, too, was unsatisfactory. He then moved to a house so remote that his parishioners complained that they could not find him. When he next moved into a bungalow in downtown Bonifacio, the place was so attractive to God's little creatures that the young priest awoke each night aware that things were walking all over him. As a result of such unpleasant housing experiences, Archbishop Cronin always advised his young priests to build a house for themselves and then a church.

What he used as the first church in Bonifacio was a roof, supported by eight wooden posts, and sides made of palm leaf and thatch. The altar was a few rough boards. No floor, no windows, no doors, no pews, no confessional, no sacristy.

He said that in those days he used to dream of a church complete with tabernacle, confessional, crucifixes, altar cloths, ciborium, monstrance, missal, vestment case, a harmonium. That seemed a lot to dream of in Mindanao.

Father Cronin soon bought four acres in the middle of Bonifacio and built a wooden church and a school. He was especially pleased with the school because the hope of the church in Mindanao was with the children.

"So many adults were indifferent after forty years without a priest," said the archbishop. "They had the faith all right. But it was what the theologians call 'the habit of faith,' and not its practical exercise."

It was in Bonifacio that Patrick Cronin learned that if he was to be "all things to all men" he would have to be sensitive to local cultures and customs. He learned the lesson so well that a young missionary said to me, "We say around here that when it comes to understanding the Filipinos, Archbishop Cronin is endowed with infallibility."

During our evening stroll (*pasao*) we usually became so engrossed in conversation that we failed to enjoy the beauty of the overhanging filigree of mimosa, the fragrance of blossoms and the night breeze in the palms. In the semidarkness children sometimes interrupted our talk, addressing the archbishop as monsignor. (In the Philippines bishops and archbishops are addressed as monsignor.) Turning from him, in his white soutane with red buttons, they gave some attention to me in my more banal suntans. They would say, "Gud-ebbening, Fadder," and bow, taking my hand and pressing it against their foreheads, a custom called the *besa*. As far as they were concerned anyone strolling in the evening with the archbishop must surely be a priest.

The archbishop said that just as he was beginning to feel at home with Filipino customs in Bonifacio the world turned topsy-turvy. On the Feast of the Immaculate Conception, December 8, 1941, he came out of the church to hear the excited parishioners repeating over and over: Pearl Harbor!

·13·

The Archbishop Remembers

The archbishop and I sat on the upstairs veranda and spoke of war. I thought of how his life had been a long, rough road from Moneygall, County Offaly, Ireland, to Cagayan de Oro, Mindanao. Providence writes such imaginative scripts!

From the veranda of the *convento*, sitting in chairs of bamboo and rattan, we looked out at a lazy curve in the Cagayan River. Coconut palms, banana plantations and dense tangle grew to the water's edge. Families came gliding down hidden paths and entered the shallow stream to bathe and wash clothes. Beyond the river a tinge of mauve made a misty outline of distant mountains.

As we sipped rum before dinner, lizards darted across the veranda ceiling in pursuit of one another, making clicking sounds all the way.

"Is that an expression of anger of or affection?" I asked.

The archbishop said that he had never been able to tell.

Affection brought young people to the banks of the river each evening. When darkness fell suddenly, as it does in the tropics, policemen sent them back to town, disrupting what the archbishop called their pre-Cana conferences.

When it was too dark to see the lizards we still heard their clicking sounds, which reminded the archbishop of the old days in Molave, a place known for its wild life: mosquitos, black ants, gnats, leeches, snakes and scorpions. Snakes were often found in the beds; scorpions hid beneath the lip of plates so that it was best to run a knife blade under each before lifting it.

From memories of Molave the talk turned to memories of war. Patrick Cronin said that when he arrived as a young priest, in 1938, Mindanao seemed too remote to fight over, but in 1942 the Japanese invaded the island. Even though the war was ugly, as wars always are, it still encouraged ingenuity and revealed courage and nobility.

In the darkness, forty years later, he described the ingenuity war demanded. His parishioners, for example, taught him to start a fire by rubbing together pieces of bamboo in a certain way. This was helpful because guerrillas used all available matches as percussion caps for rifle ammunition. The shells were segments of curtain rods stuffed with dynamite, amatol and firecracker powder. Lead bullets were fashioned from fishermen's sinkers. Such rifles sometimes blew sky high.

The Filipinos used tough vines for shoestrings, and they carved buttons from coconut shells. They made clothing from hemp fiber and turned banana leaves, six feet long and three wide, into rainwear.

The Japanese caused shortages of everything because they lived off the land and even shipped food to Tokyo. A Filipino farmer complained: "Before war we fat hog today so we can die hog tomorrow. Now can't fat hog. No hog. Work he is so many; chow she is so few."

Food was often unsavory. The archbishop recalled the time an American dined with a Moro whose sullen wife did not want to prepare the meal. She thrust at him a filthy pot filled with ill-cooked brown mountain rice in which nestled little legs, arms and hands. It gave off a gamey stench. Monkey.

A couple of hundred Americans, left trapped on the island, turned to guerrilla warfare. Their leader, Colonel Wendell Fertig, had been a rumor well before Father Cronin met him. Everybody and everything that did not fit the prevailing pattern became rumors. All news was reduced to gossip that flew swiftly "from mouth to ear," as the Filipinos say, a form of communication known as the bamboo telegraph.

Patrick Cronin recalled the day an excited parishioner came running up the steps of the veranda shouting that Colonel Fertig was on his way. Minutes later the colonel stood framed in the doorway. His khakis seemed more starched than they really were because he stood straight and tall. The missionary observed that his guest had close-cropped sandy hair and a neatly trimmed goatee. The colonel greeted the priest with a warm handshake and said, "Don't let things get you down, Father." The colonel's visits helped keep up Patrick Cronin's morale. Night after night they sat in the rattan chairs surrounded by heat, chirring locusts and the densely jungled hills.

Colonel Fertig had been ordered out of Corregidor to join General MacArthur's headquarters in Australia. The first airplane that was to lift him from the Rock crashed on landing there. He boarded the second and escaped uninjured when it crashed on takeoff. Through a confusion of orders he missed the submarine that was to evacuate him. Finally he escaped on the last Navy flying boat to leave Corregidor before the surrender, but never reached Australia because the flying boat crashed on Lake Lanao in Mindanao.

Fertig felt he had been spared for a special assignment. His sense of mission was more easily admitted to a priest than to his fellow soldiers.

He wrote in his diary: "God, you've helped me this far. Thank you for the help. I'll try to do the best I can, and I hope you'll want to go on helping me. God, if it is my fate to tell other people what to do, please help me to guess right."

Later he wrote: "During the months in the forest, I have become acquainted with myself and developed a feeling I do not walk alone, a feeling that a Power greater than any human power has my destiny in hand. Like a swimmer, carried forward by a powerful current, I can direct my course as long as my way lies in the direction of the irresistible flow of events."

Colonel Fertig told Father Cronin that had it not been for a Columban missionary, Father Thomas Callanan, he might not have had the courage to take on the awesome task of a guerilla leader. The colonel had asked the priest if he could depend on the support of the Church should he try to organize the Filipinos into a fighting force. The young pastor of Jimenez, who had come to Mindanao with Patrick Cronin, explained that officially the Church was neutral. But unofficially it was against what the Japanese stood for because they said that they intended to drive Americans and their beliefs from East Asia. A Japanese official had boasted to a Filipino priest: "No more Jesus Christ. All now belong Nippon."

One night Father Callanan and Colonel Fertig, both gentlemen of sparkling courtesy, were guests at a dinner given by the leading political family of Mindanao, the Ozamis family of Jimenez. When Dona Carmen, the head of the house, spoke of the possibilities of an effective resistance movement, she looked carefully at the Irish priest. Fertig always believed that she gave her approval after seeing that the missionary was at least not opposed. The real guerrilla movement was born that night in Casa Ozamis, Fertig said.

With the help of 200 Americans who had escaped Japanese internment, he formed an army of 35,000 Filipinos.

The archbishop told me that one of Fertig's men developed a radio of sorts, a Rube Goldberg device that somehow worked. Day after day the signal officer tapped out a one-sentence message that he hoped would make contact with an American station and attract a reply. He thought that the sentence, "We have the hot dope on the hot Yanks in the hot Philippines" sounded very American. At the receiving end in San Francisco everybody agreed that it had the faked sound of a Japanese message, and so refrained from answering.

This frustration was the final straw for three American officers. They decided to travel the 1,400 miles between Mindanao and Australia to report what was happening and to ask for aid.

With money borrowed from Father Cronin and a few other people, they went to the port of Bonifacio to buy a twenty-six-foot craft with a defective Japanese diesel engine.

"After much preparation," the archbishop said, "and many delays due to engine trouble and lack of fuel and oil, they were ready to sail in December 1942. In this small boat with only a mining compass and a National Geographic map of the southwest Pacific, which I gave them, they sailed for Australia. I also gave them a small edition of the New Testament."

The three Americans sailed the seas of the southwest Pacific replenishing water and supplies at tiny islands where the enemy was not apt to be found. Even though the Japanese had landed in Borneo, the Celebes, Sumatra, Java and other islands between Mindanao and Australia, and patrolled the waters with destroyers, corvettes and launches, the only time the Americans were in real trouble was when they were chased by an enemy launch just north of New Guinea. After twenty-five days at sea the little boat reached a lighthouse north of Darwin.

When a submarine surfaced at the Mindanao port of Bonifacio, weeks later, Captain Charles Smith hurried from it to find Father Cronin, saying, "I came to pay back what I owe you. And by the way here is some Mass wine."

The submarine brought supplies good for morale but also brought news hard to accept—the realization that "the aid" would not be coming for a long time. Before the arrival of the submarine everyone spoke of "the aid," meaning American troops storming ashore to drive the Japanese from Mindanao.

Now they heard that when MacArthur had arrived in Australia he learned that the Philippines were near the bottom of the list in the big strategy. The Germans were overrunning Europe, chasing the Russians eastward and also doing well in North Africa. The Japanese had things their way in China and in Burma and threatened India. Colonel Fertig's barefoot Filipino fighters could consider themselves expendable.

Before Captain Smith had sailed for Australia, Fertig gave him a radio signal known only to the two of them: MSF—meaning Mindanao, Smith, Fertig. After he reached Australia he told the station in San Francisco to send the prearranged signal. Father Cronin and Fertig were standing at the wireless on the dark and rainy night, February 2, 1943, when the signal came through. From then on there was contact with Washington and with MacArthur's headquarters in Australia. This, too, was good for morale.

Father Cronin was pleased when a radio message came awarding Fertig the Distinguished Service Cross. The message was from MacArthur and bore the congratulations of president Manuel Quezon.

From then on wherever Fertig went the Filipinos greeted him in a way that made his travels something of a movable feast. In Tangub, Father Cronin's former parishioners welcomed the guerrilla leader with such affection that it brought tears to his eyes. Fishermen and their families, dressed in their *fiesta* best, held aloft coconut-oil lamps to light the way for the outrigger to bring Fertig to their shore. Accompanied by three guitars, an accordion and a violin, they sang, "Somm whaare ovva de rain-bow . . ."

The submarine had also brought a message from MacArthur that said in effect: Quit trying to kill Japanese; gather information instead. Establish a flash line of watching stations along the coast. Submarines will intercept the enemy ships that you report.

Fertig ordered his guerrillas to surround and protect strategic observation stations. Transmitters had arrived by submarine and a few more were built. The Filipinos kept batteries charged with water wheels, cornmills, foot chargers and auto chargers.

The system worked. Father Callanan was aware of how well it worked when he was passing through a market, one day in May 1943, and heard the cry "Japanese! Japanese!" Down the road came a dozen Japanese prisoners. Their officer, who spoke English well, told the priest that two of their ships had been sunk.

Scarcely a week went by without someone witnessing a sinking off the coast of Mindanao. Those thousands of eyes on the hills reported all movements of enemy ships and flights of enemy planes. With the help of the Mindanao network the Japanese fleet was destroyed by the United States Navy off the Marianas.

Besides gathering information, Fertig's guerrillas kept 150,000 Japanese from feeling free to go to other islands where serious fighting was in progress. In time, General Morimoto, the Japanese commander, decided to put an end to such annoyances, and planned Operation Big Voice with the mission of silencing Fertig's radios and killing Fertig himself. The plan did not succeed because double agents reported all of this to guerrilla headquarters.

During this time Father Patrick Cronin came near death on several occasions. One midnight Fertig burst into his *convento* urging him to hurry to the hills: "The Japs have landed and are coming up the road fast. You had better clear out!"

Earlier in the day Fertig had said: "The jungle is bad and no place for any man. But it is to be preferred to the Japs."

That observation was affirmed by a sentence in a missionary's diary: "Near Imbatug I buried people sawed in two."

One night, while on the run, Father Cronin went to sleep in a house half hidden by dwarf coconut trees. The Japanese entered several houses a few yards away. Perhaps his was missed because it was dark while the others, because of the children in them, kept coconut oil burning through the night.

Years later the archbishop told me of another close call: "I looked down the hill and saw a Japanese patrol walking along the valley road in the direction I wanted to go. So I followed well behind them on horseback. Things went well until my return trip when I met a young Filipino and we went along the road together. Suddenly, he stopped and said he was turning back. He saw the tips of three rifles sticking above the tall grass a few yards ahead.

"I didn't see them. My eyes haven't been too good since seminary days. But I had not time to doubt the accuracy of his observation. Something like a buzzing bee went past.

"I kicked my heels into the horse's side. A sitting target. At full gallop I jumped off and rolled into the tall grass. The density of the underbush was such that I had to get down on hands and knees to penetrate it. Exhausted, I rolled into a hole only to find it filled with black ants.

"My glasses were missing! The only pair I owned. I couldn't bear to think of going through the war without glasses. So I crawled back, and there they were in the middle of the road. Inch by inch I eased out to regain them.

"How regain the horse? Especially the saddle. I climbed a tree to get directions. After fording a river I came to a *barrio* where they had caught the runaway. They had heard the shot and when they saw the riderless horse galloping along and recognized it they cried, 'The padre is dead! The padre is dead!' The news raced through the hills. Wherever I went for weeks I had to explain why I was still alive."

From the three tons of equipment on that first submarine to reach Mindanao, the tonnage increased until eventually the largest sub in the world, the *U.S.S. Narwhal*, brought in ninety tons of supplies. The archbishop said that time and again submarine commanders offered priests and nuns a chance to escape on return trips to Australia, but all preferred to stay in Mindanao. Knowing this the Filipinos developed an affection for the missionaries that carried over into peacetime.

·14·

Growth in Mindanao

I would have felt at ease with Patrick Cronin before the war when he spent hours walking through the close, endless monotony of forest or riding horseback over miles of empty trails. That would have suited me better than the 1976 rides in his car, lurching across bad roads surrounded by noisy, defective motors, honking horns and choking dust. Drivers hurtled through space, for to go more slowly would mean a loss of "face." There was a sign: "God's Country, Don't Drive Like Hell," but most drivers were going too fast to read it.

Yet amid such commotion we were surrounded by saints. The San Pedro rice mill, the Lourdes beauty parlor and the Immaculate Conception pharmacy were along the way. Hundreds of children, poorly clad or naked, swarmed from the *barrios* to greet us, bearing such names as Francisca, Noberta, Mateo, Marciano and Apollania. Once I saw a bus from the San Antonio Service Line narrowly escape colliding with a truck displaying across its hood the supplication, "Holy Mary Pray for Me," and well she might.

To visit Ozamis, where Patrick Cronin did most of his work after the war, I took a small plane from Cagayan de Oro southwest across Iligan Bay. Considering the size of the craft the pilot flew at a fairly high altitude and in approaching the landing field dove for it. Since the cabin lacked pressure control, the rapid descent brought the agony of daggers piercing the inner ear. Perhaps the pilot was used to it; perhaps he enjoyed watching the Americano flinch.

In Ozamis I stayed in a rambling two-story structure that serves as Columban headquarters, rest center and retreat house. Nearby, on Iligan Bay, a long barracks and a few nipa huts are the dormitories and the classrooms of the language school started by Patrick Cronin when he became bishop of Ozamis.

Because of the ineptness of language study in Mindanao, the bishop arranged that newly arriving priests and nuns have six months of courses before being sent on assignment. After a year they return for a refresher course of six weeks. Then back into the field for two more years before returning for a final six weeks at the language school.

But that is getting ahead of the story.

After the war, Father Cronin spent a few hard years starting a parish in remote Salug, in the province of Zamboanga. Salug had a reputation of being the most difficult assignment in Mindanao. The Malindang Mountains and the Midsalip Ranges are rugged; the Salug, Mahayag and Guitran rivers have a habit of flooding. All manner of insects thrive in a country that seems to be either dense with forests or deep with mud. To make the missionary's life harder the parish is strung out across vast distances with dozens of *barrios* reached by slippery mountain trails where two steps forward are followed by a slip backward.

The name of Salug was eventually changed to Molave, but as Salug it had developed a notoriety that reached as far as the seminary in Ireland, where the very mention of the name brought a shiver. So when a young priest, Father James Mulroy, who had not heard about the change of name, was told that he would be a curate in Molave, he sighed, "Thank God it's not Salug!"

Father Cronin found his parishioners in Molave as sturdy as the molave tree which has lumber so tough it defies the sharp-toothed termite, so strong it supports heavy loads, and so heavy that it sinks in water.

Indomitable Molave farmers, with nothing more than the family water buffalo, crossed rivers, penetrated the uplands and cleared land to plant rice and corn. Lacking axes and horses, they could not hack down and haul away primeval trees and so they burned them, leaving blackened stumps to rot away with time. The farmers plowed around the stumps and planted seed. When foliage no longer blocked the sun a harvest of sorts developed.

Every village in the hills built its own chapel of bamboo and palm leaves. Since Father Cronin wanted to visit each village once a month he spent much time in the saddle.

The archbishop told me, with feeling, about Midsalip, one of his outstations, a village twenty-five miles from the nearest road. Not even a horse could get there. When visiting his parishioners in that remote place, the missionary left the road and headed into the forest. It meant a day of hiking and climbing to an extensive plateau about 2,000 feet above sea level. Only a local guide could find the trail that led through thick woods and heavy undergrowth, a way blocked with fallen trees.

Years later the archbishop used to tell newly arrived young priests, "Don't say you have been on the missions until you see Midsalip."

At age thirty-eight Patrick Cronin became a monsignor. Archbishop Hayes, of Cagayan, installed him as apostolic administrator of the new diocese of Ozamis on May 20, 1952. The title of apostolic administrator means that he would be performing all functions of a bishop except that of ordaining priests.

To attend the installation, 2,000 parishioners packed the wood-and-concrete cathedral in Ozamis City. Ninety priests crowded the sanctuary.

In his sermon that day, Archbishop Hayes quoted some statistics that the monsignor found impressive. The Columbans had increased their number of priests in Mindanao from the original ten in 1938 to forty in 1952 and their parishes from nine to twenty. Where there had been but one Catholic school there were now fifteen, plus three colleges, the largest of which, with 1,200 students, was conducted by Columban Sisters in Ozamis City. The growth was remarkable, observed Archbishop Hayes, since it happened in only thirteen years, four of which were filled with war.

Monsignor Cronin learned, in the sermon that morning, that within his new diocese would be 300,000 Catholics and 320,000 non-Catholics, some of whom were schismatic, some Protestant, but most Muslim. The numbers frightened him. He looked back on his hard life in Bonafacio and Molave and it all seemed simple compared with this.

Years later he said to me, "Soon you learn that each day brings events that lead to a clearer understanding of what is *really* needed. So you gradually grow from neophyte to old hand."

When Patrick Cronin became a bishop, three years later, he felt that the most pressing need was for more priests. On the occasion of his consecration at the Columban seminary, in Navan, he told the many priests who had gathered for the ceremony about the lack of priests in the Philippines.

Soon after returning to Mindanao the bishop began writing articles for the three Columban magazines published in Ireland, Australia and the United States, telling the story in many dramatic ways: "Several parishes with four to seven priests in pastoral work are listed in the Philippine Catholic Directory as having 62,000, 73,000, 87,000, 90,000 and even 120,000! I doubt if similar figures can be found in any other part of the Catholic world."

By the time I came to know Patrick Cronin, the growth of a native-born clergy had provided him with brighter statistics. At the time he became Archbishop of Cagayan de Oro, in 1970, he wrote: "Many new seminaries have developed in the Philippines since the war. Now in the fourteen major seminaries there are 1,012 students and the 31 minor seminaries cater to 3,147 students."

On one of our evening strolls, four times around the park for a mile, the archbishop spoke with feeling about how the Columbans are fighting a numbers battle. He said that throughout the islands there are 233 Columban priests and that sounds like quite a few until you consider the other statistics: They serve ninety-six parishes and thousands of *barrio* chapels. They are in charge of 117 elementary and secondary schools and 15 colleges with a total enrollment of 60,000 students.

Patience is the virtue that has kept Patrick Cronin going through the years. The advice he gives concerning patience is much the same as the old Archbishop of Manila, Michael J. O'Doherty, used to give. He would point to a *carabao* lumbering along swinging its heavy horns, something of a primeval, irresistible force. After a dramatic pause he would say to the newly arrived missionary: "Consider the *carabao*; study his ways; learn from him. He moves slowly, slowly, slowly. But he gets there just the same."

Archbishop Cronin preached patience to the young missionaries—patience with the people, patience with the situation and patience with yourself.

Each evening I felt that the archbishop needed to remind himself to be patient when time came for supper and we moved from the dark veranda to the yellow light of the dining room where there were almost sure to be several guests at the table. The archbishop said to me, "People say, 'You have a big house here,' as though that is a great luxury. It would be a great luxury to have a small house. If a bishop wanted to be selfish he would live in a humble house with his office some distance away and he would keep office hours, as most professional men do. When you have a big house—certainly on the missions—it is filled with visitors most of the time. You get no privacy. No rest. It's best though to keep the big house open to all the priests. They need a place to come to."

As an outsider I found the table talk interesting. For instance, a young Filipino priest had just come in from some remote part of the diocese, thin and worn. The archbishop asked, "You need any money?" The young priest looked shy and said, no. "Are you getting enough to eat?" The young priest nodded, yes.

Little by little everyone at the table told his troubles: Someone is trying to poison the well in the *barrio* . . . a plague of locusts is destroying the crops . . . an ex-nun has been arrested on charges of radical activity.

Some of the anecdotes were on the lighter side: A missionary wondered why the big holy-water font at the back of his church was empty each evening, even though he filled it at noon. He found the answer when he caught a parishioner's horse drinking from it.

This animal anecdote reminded another missionary to tell of his experiences with rats. Most nights he is awakened by something brushing against his hand or cheek. In the dim light of the flashlight there is a scurry throughout the room. He has taken to shooting his guests with a rifle.

For me, a writer working on a book, this was all wonderful stuff. But I could tell by looking at the archbishop that sometimes he would be thinking of what a great luxury it would be to dine alone.

When I was returning to the States, Archbishop Cronin came as far as Manila with me. Shortly before my plane was to depart he finally told me the story of how his father had been shot down in front of the family home in Tullamore.

The archbishop said he hoped to return to Ireland the following summer. I promised to meet him there with the finished manuscript.

In Killiney, in the summer of 1977, he zipped through the pages of his life's story with remarkable rapidity, for he can almost read a page at a glance. As I recall, he asked for only one change: Substitute the word crow for monkey.

This had to do with a nickname that Sister Breda, a Columban, earned in Ozamis. It was given to her by Mr. Siao, an ancient Filipino. She had discovered him lying on the bamboo floor of a tiny room, a bent tin mug at his side and a clutter of papers all around. She noticed a dirty bandage wrapped around his left hand and could smell the diseased wound it covered. He was alone, diabetic and with a sore already showing signs of gangrene.

After the nun took steps to have him cared for, Mr. Siao began hanging around the clinic, making comments. One day as he sat watching her work he said quite unexpectedly, "You are humanity." But that was not how she got the nickname.

It came when Mr. Siao was confronted by a young Filipino nurse who accused him of never following instructions. He grumbled around the rest of the morning and complained to Sister Breda that the young nurse was a "wise monkey," a title not complimentary in the Philippines.

The expression so amused the nun that she repeated it often in Mr. Siao's presence. It became an "in" joke between them. Then it was that he endowed Sister Breda with the nickname: Head of the Wise Monkeys.

The archbishop felt uneasy about the anecdote, explaining that when American soldiers sang, "Oh, the monkeys have no tails in Zamboanga," the Filipinos believed the soldiers were singing about them. So he asked that I change Wise Monkey to Wise Crow.

This sensitivity of the archbishop's reminded me of the time the young missionary had said to me, "We say around here that when it comes to understanding the Filipinos, Archbishop Cronin is endowed with infallibility."

In Ireland the archbishop and I resumed our evening strolls. Now it was along the strand of the Irish Sea in Killiney Bay. Perhaps it was seeing his life's story on paper that caused him to marvel, as had Archbishop Henry, at the mysterious ways of Providence.

"A series of coincidences put me in this position," he said. "It's beyond my competence and ability. And somehow I am surviving! I was only an average student. Nobody foresaw I would be put into this position. Certainly I didn't. Only through coincidence. Take for instance how I happened to be in Cagayan de Oro. The old archbishop decided to retire. His coadjutor, with the right to succession, decided to resign at the same time. Pure coincidence!"

Even as he stressed the word coincidence, walking along the sandy strand, he was aware of the mystery of grace. In working on the biography he had become impressed by how God breaks into life in new and startling ways. It made him aware of how the Almighty is the author of the unexpected, and that his ways of running the world are more interesting than ours.

The archbishop told me he found satisfaction in sticking it out. He had endured all of those rough years. It always surprised him. He hoped the old Irish missionary was right when he said: "In heaven I don't expect credit for coming on the mission. Ah, no! But I hope I get credit for staying."

The last time I saw Archbishop Cronin was again in Ireland and quite by chance. He and his sister, Peggy, came to the Columban seminary in County Meath, in the fall of 1979, where I was finishing the manuscript of another book.

They each spoke with enthusiasm about *Mindanao Mission*.

I remembered, but not out loud, how opposed the archbishop had been to having his biography written three years earlier. Perhaps when he saw the words on paper he realized that it would be a shame not to have the story told.

·15·

Burma Days

In May of 1945 I was living in Bhamo. When asked where I wanted to settle down to write the story of the war in northern Burma I said, "Some place where nobody will bother me." I meant a tent for myself in a jungle clearing, but the United States Army, with larger plans, assigned me a deserted Buddhist monastery on the banks of the Irrawaddy. The monks had fled when the war arrived. For meals I walked down a shell-pocked trail to an elongated bamboo structure that served as an officers' mess.

One noon early in May I saw a tall, lean man pause at the mess-hall door to survey the shabby room. He had in his face and manner "the look of eagles." Since he wore GI suntans I took for granted that he was an officer, although he wore no insignia. A lack of it was usual in Burma; Japanese snipers looked for insignia when deciding at whom to aim, and so signs of rank were often omitted.

I saw the stranger for less than five seconds; he never saw me, but he stayed in my memory through the decades. Then one day in 1977 when working in the Columban archives in Killiney I came upon a photograph of him: Patrick Usher.

I hurried downstairs to tell Father William Kehoe, with whom I used to walk around Killiney, in the long Celtic twilights, recalling our Burma days. He had never come right out and said that I ought to put it all down on paper, but it was on his mind. Now that I was speaking with such enthusiasm, he gave me one of his crooked smiles, knowing I was stuck from now on: I could not rest until telling the story of Monsignor Patrick Usher's life in Burma. Here again was an example of a small incident giving life a definite direction. There are no coincidences, said Jung, the psychiatrist, and that I firmly believe. Such happenings are providential.

In testing my willingness to face up to doing another book about missionaries, Father Kehoe said that the government of Burma would not welcome me there. He added that fortunately, of all the places in the world that the United States Army could have sent me during the war, it had providentially chosen Myitkyina and Bhamo, the two towns to which Columban missionaries had given most attention. Since I had lived in those places, and now with research in the archives and interviews with old Burma hands, I should be able to tell the story, he said.

That evening as Father Kehoe and I walked along Killiney Bay I asked how the Columbans happened to go to the remoteness of northern Burma. Such a God-forsaken place!

"Rumors about Burma were plentiful when I was ordained at Christmas of 1935," he said. "The twenty-five of us in that class continued to study while waiting for an appointment. Word went around that the Columbans would undertake another mission—in addition to those in China, Korea and the Philippines."

Months passed and rumors intensified, until one morning in May the class president, Father Thomas Murphy, moved among his friends in the lecture hall, placing a hand on each of five shoulders, saying, "You are appointed to the new mission in Burma." He, too, would be with them, he said.

The young men were pleased to hear that Father Patrick Usher would also be going to Burma as their superior. At the seminary they had come to admire the thirty-six-year-old Usher, a tall man with quick, energetic movements, sharp features and sandy hair as resilient as wire.

Since his ordination, a dozen years earlier, Father Usher had been the seminary's business manager, a tame assignment for a man who enjoyed adventure. Now his characteristic impatience came bubbling up and he announced that he would sail in September, a month before the other priests.

Father Usher and Father Bernard Way reached Burma at dawn on October 21, 1936. Their steamer stopped to pick up the harbor pilot in the wide, muddy expanse of sea where the Irrawaddy empties into the ocean. The boat churned yellow water cluttered with scum, flotsam and water hyacinths. Gradually, Rangoon took form in the mist, its flatness and drabness relieved only by the golden, gleaming spire of the Shwe Dagon pagoda.

The Columbans boarded a narrow-gauge railroad for the first step of the 750-mile journey from Rangoon to Bhamo. The tiny engine chugged along for eighteen hours across the flat, alluvial plain, one of the richest rice fields in the world.

The two priests stopped in Mandalay to meet with Bishop Albert Faliere. At the station an effervescent Frenchman and a more sedate Burman, both wearing white soutanes, greeted the Columbans. As the Frenchman rushed about searching for baggage, Father Usher asked the Burman where Bishop Faliere might be. The Burman nodded toward the Frenchman pulling trunks out of the railroad carriage.

Bishop Faliere was a member of the Foreign Mission Society of Paris, the Society that had asked the Columbans to come to Burma because it lacked missionaries. The war that had raged in Europe from August 1914 until November of 1918 took the lives of so many young Frenchman that now there was a shortage of priests.

As far as Fathers Usher and Way were concerned the Foreign Mission Society of Paris was "the big league" in mission work. So many of its priests came out for life, while they, Columbans, were looking forward to a visit home in ten years.

The Columbans were touched by such anecdotes as the one about the old French missionary who served in a remote part of Burma without going home for fifty-seven years. When he heard that a confrere was on his way to Paris, he wrote: "When you return to France, call at my home and kiss for me the little Annette." He remembered his sister as she had been at age seven on the day of his ordination. When the priest returned to Burma, he did not have the heart to tell his compatriot that when he went to deliver the message, it was an old woman who raised her cheek to be kissed.

Right off the Columbans took a liking to Bishop Faliere, an excellent companion and a tour guide beyond compare. He insisted on accompanying them on their four-day riverboat trip up the Irrawaddy to Bhamo.

On the way the bishop pointed out how north of Mandalay the country turns into rocky bluffs covered with tangled jungle and tall elephant grass. The Columbans were pleased by the picturesqueness of little villages rambling along the bank of the river with long flights of steps descending through dark green foliage to the water's edge.

Soon mountains moved in close to form the Irrawaddy defile. Above Katha the Irrawaddy began looking more like a river and less like a series of lakes. The mountains came in exceedingly close to create the gateway to Kachin country, the land where the Columbans would work out their destiny.

Once more the mountains receded until the landscape spread out, making way for open plains. The boat slowed down and swung completely around toward a crude jetty floating in the stream. Three French priests stood waiting on the low brown bank. The end of the journey: Bhamo.

A month after arriving in Bhamo, Fathers Usher and Way went down to the insubstantial jetty on the Irrawaddy to welcome six young priests fresh from home. They helped load suitcases and bedrolls onto three creaking bullock carts and then walked two miles over a dusty road to Bhamo Town.

Darkness came down fast as the journey neared its end. More than forty years later one of the priests would recall: "We were greeted at our unimposing mission house by a solitary French priest, Father François Collard. He bore a smoking lamp. It shed little light on a very dark scene."

Although the young priests did not comment on the darkness of the scene, Father Usher knew how they felt. A few days earlier he had admitted to Father Way: "The first night in Bhamo my heart went down to my boots. When I saw this old dilapidated house I said to myself, 'What is the rest like!'"

What lifted Patrick Usher's spirits was his first visit with Father Charles Gilhodes in a village called Hkudung, 3,000 feet above Bhamo. The Columban wrote, "He was alone in a part of the country which must rank high among the lonely places of the world."

When the old French priest heard that two new missionaries wished to visit him, he sent down a guide with ponies. This form of transportation was new to Father Usher.

"My pony reached almost to my hip," he wrote, "and it seemed brutal to mount him. I was amazed at the sure-footed ease with which the little animal carried me upward for two and a half hours. I was grateful, too, for his smooth steady pace. Small though he was, he had a dignity of his own and did not grudge me mine."

The two Columbans took delight in the six-mile ride up and up. The path, scarcely a yard wide, clung to a steep incline, curving and twisting all the way. On the right the jungle towered; on the left a stream hurried through the valley. From all sides came incessant buzzing, a background to occasional bird calls—the voice of the jungle.

In that remote village, the visitors were surprised to find a thousand Catholics. They also found the Franciscan Missionaries of Mary operating an orphanage and school for about 300 children and a dispensary that treated fifty cases a day. These were the nuns Father Gilhodes spoke of years later when receiving the Order of the British Empire. Asked on that occasion what was the greatest gift he had brought to the Kachins, the old missionary answered, "The Sisters."

The children of Hkudung were out to meet the two Columbans as they came riding into the village. In their own brand of English they extended greetings, and the smallest of the lot stepped forward to hand Father Usher a letter that he treasured:

> Dear Rev. Fathers,
> We the people of Kachin Hills, old, yeng, thin and fat are all gathered hear today to pay our best wishes to you, which gushes out from the bottom of our hearts. We are very glad to see our good shepherds who have come to tend the flock of the Kachin Hills from a far noble country.

The date, November 4, 1936, was the feast of the pastor, who made sure that the celebration was not focused on himself. He had the parishioners so arrange the festivities that it would seem everyone had gathered just for the visit of the Columbans.

The welcoming ceremony took place in front of the boarding school, a warren of wooden buildings with zinc roofs, and all higgledy-piggledy. Here a classroom was stuck on and there a dormitory was attached to a dining room but at a different level. Stairways and verandas ran up and down and back and forth at various plateaus. Among all of this visual to-do, more than 200 boarders were getting an education.

In this remote spot, 3,401 feet above sea level, Father Charles Gilhodes had arrived in 1903 suffering indifferent health and totally ignorant of the Kachin language. In a small hut in the village he lived for thirteen years without a convert.

"What did you do all of that time?" asked Father Usher.

"I said the rosary."

In addition to praying he made a close study of the Kachin language and customs, the basis of his book which, in France, was widely acclaimed for its scholarship. Gradually the barriers came down. The opening wedge was a special French dictionary, one that showed a little sketch of everything that could be illustrated.

He would start with the children, he thought, for they seemed to have nothing to do. He would teach them while they taught him.

The start was disappointing. The children had never seen a white man, nor one so bearded, nor one wearing such a strange white robe. When he approached, they ran.

Father Usher asked the frail old man, "How did you gain their confidence?" He was thinking of the hundreds of bright-faced children who had just greeted them.

"Bon bons," said Father Gilhodes. "I went to the nearest large village and bought a box of them. The next time the children fled I threw a handful of bon bons and withdrew and waited. Before many days they were coming to meet me.''

The language lesson began with the simple objects seen all about: houses, trees, hills, chickens, dogs. Each sound was patiently noted down and memorized. Little by little the French priest and the Kachin children traded vocabularies.

Father Gilhodes decided that disease was rampant among the Kachins because of an unbalanced diet. He wrote for seeds to Europe and India and several countries in Southeast Asia. By experimenting he found which took most kindly to Kachin soil. Eventually, when orchards and gardens grew there was a noticeable drop in disease and in infant mortality.

How might the Kachins earn enough income to allow for a dignified standard of living? Father Gilhodes grappled with that one for a long time. When he sponsored the first coffee and tea plantation on Kachin land, he opened a new chapter in Kachin history.

That visit to Father Gilhodes was just what Patrick Usher needed. The feeling of defeat that had oppressed him that first night in Bhamo was somewhat dispelled. His morale climbed higher each time he climbed into the hills. The affection he was developing for Burma and its people shows in a letter he wrote home:

> Travel is absolutely gorgeous in the part of the country I have seen. We have three towns in a territory the size of Ireland. They are linked together by either rail or river, and for some miles around each of them there is a bus service. After that you take to your feet or your pony and immediately all the troubles of civilization drop from you. No more post or telegraph or other messages to recall you. You may wear what you like, and think, say, sing, or do what you like.

As Father Usher walked along, or rode his pony, he kept an eye out for a likely place to establish a mission church. Some promising spots were vacant because a house there had been destroyed by fire. When that happens the Kachins believe an evil spirit abides on the spot and no one will build on it while the memory remains. Sites considered unlucky are given to Catholic priests for mission stations, Father Gilhodes had said.

Fortunately, Father Usher had lifted his own morale before he conducted the first spiritual retreat ever given in the Kachin Hills. During it he spoke at length to the young priests about the difficulties the French missionaries had endured and quoted from Ecclesiasticus: "My son, if you aspire to serve the Lord, prepare for an ordeal."

He brought the retreat to a close with words that he lived by during all of his years in Burma: "I know that God gives his grace in proportion to the work He asks us to do. If I didn't believe that I would shrink from the task.

"We are a small rather helpless bunch of inexperienced missionaries. We know little of the language and less of the customs of our people. In a human way we have nothing to recommend us or guarantee any measure of success. But we do, or at least ought to, possess a mighty weapon of the spirit—Charity. Love. If we have that, God's work will prosper. If we haven't that, let's pack up our bags and go home!"

When the retreat ended the young priests were in better spirits but painfully aware of the many things they needed to learn—the language, the customs of the people, the religions of the tribes.

It was a humbling experience, for instance, to be classified as illiterate after twenty years of schooling. The Columbans laughed, but cringed a little, when a Burmese census taker wrote in his report: "Two Catholic priests, both illiterate." So the eight illiterate Columbans began steeping themselves in languages.

The country was still part of the British Empire, but English was seldom spoken except by foreigners and officials. Of the 130 languages Burmese was the one used by government-aided schools and by the more sophisticated people of lower Burma. In remote upper Burma, where the Columbans worked, the principal languages were Shan and Kachin.

Although the missionaries would have little use for Burmese, Patrick Usher felt he needed some facility with the official language, and so he and Father McAlindon went to a village near Mandalay to study. Three of the priests studied Shan in Nanghlaing and three studied Kachin in Hkudung. No Columban studied the language of the Nagas, a hill tribe of headhunters who believe that evil spirits destroy a rice crop unless fresh heads are impaled on bamboo poles and set in the village as a token of respect for the spirits.

Languages of the Far East are awkward for Western tongues. The missionaries found Shan more difficult than Kachin because of its subtle tonal demands. A word may be spoken in five different tones, each giving it a different meaning. *Seu* is tiger, if said with a even sound. Said gruffly it means straight. Sung at a high level and stretched out it says happy. Sung high in a staccato it means buy.

In Kachin there are also tonal problems—not so great, but great enough to cause embarrassment on occasion. For example, when an animist, a religious leader called a *dumsa* in Kachin, joined the Church, the Columban repeatedly referred to him in a short talk as a big *dumsu*. Each time the convert flinched because *dumsu* means cow.

Father Gilhodes taught the Columbans about the religion of Kachins. They are not, he said, attracted to Buddhism, as are the Shans, and so in all of the hill country not a pagoda is to be seen. The Kachins do not have an organized religion but rather a collection of customs.

As animists, the Kachins believe in spirits called *nats*. Every aspect of life has its particular *nat*. One presides over health and one over disease; one is for a good harvest and another for a bad one. The *nats* most feared are *jahtung*, those who bring bad luck in hunting and fishing; *sawn*, those who cause women to die in childbirth, and *lasa*, those who cause accidental deaths. To assuage such evil spirits a buffalo, ox or fowl might be slaughtered. A succession of misfortunes could in no time deplete a family's livestock.

All of this concern with the world of spirits, Father Gilhodes said, should make Kachins ready to accept the message of Christianity. Father Usher agreed and wrote home, "The doctrine of the loving providence of God should appeal to tribesmen burdened with a fear of malignant *nats*."

And so it happened, but it took time.

·16·

Off to the Hills

A chill from wet clothing developed into double pneumonia after Father Usher had been caught in a downpour while hiking in the hills on a cold windy day. He lay seriously ill for three months, until Christmas of 1937.

The happy side of that unpleasant time was that six more missionaries had been sent out from home and another six would soon arrive. Besides, Bhamo was about to become a prefecture apostolic and Patrick Usher would become a monsignor.

By now he was sure that the Columbans should focus attention on the Kachins rather than the Shans. The tribesmen occupied the great series of hills stretching across northern Burma into China's Yunnan Province. The borders between the countries wandered in and out among the hills so erratically that at some places it was impossible to decide whether you were in Burma or China. Monsignor Usher hoped that, in time, the Columbans might link up with missionaries on the China side, the Betharram Fathers from the south of France.

But why open new territory at this time? Why not develop Myitkyina, a town 100 miles above Bhamo, easily reached by train or by boat. The argument haunted the monsignor until he went up to survey the possibilities.

Sixteen years later he wrote: "At that time we owned a half-acre of land in Myitkyina on which there was a two-room house for the priest and a small church for a handful of Catholics. A priest used to come by train once a month to say Mass for them."

To give Myitkyina more attention made sense, and yet there was that nagging need to open new territory. He wrote later: "The thing that stands out clearest in my memory was the feeling of dismay."

Patrick Usher felt drawn to the Triangle, a vast, wild, mountainous tract north of Myitkyina. It has the shape of a triangle because two rivers, the Mali and the N'mai, start 60 miles apart up near the Himalayas in Tibet, and tend toward each other during the 120-mile journey south. When they join they form the Irrawaddy, which continues down the center of Burma past Myitkyina, Bhamo and Mandalay to reach the sea at Rangoon.

Although England had been controlling parts of Burma since 1826, the British made no attempt to put the Triangle under civil administration until 1927, less than a decade before the Columbans arrived. Perhaps they would never have bothered that remote wilderness, except that slavery was practiced there. When the government tried freeing the slaves through negotiation, local chieftains said the British Raj should stop tampering with traditional rights.

In March of 1927, the government sent a detachment of military police, mostly Indian Ghurkas, under command of Captain Maxwell West, to arrange terms for freeing slaves. Upon entering the Triangle, the police began reconstructing a bridge only to find themselves caught in an ambush. Captain West and a Kachin leader were killed and several villages were destroyed by fire.

Soon the Kachin guerrillas disbanded and the chiefs agreed to release slaves if the government would pay for them. The rate settled on was 10 rupees for children, 120 for maidens and young men, and 60 for older people. (A rupee in those days was worth about thirty cents.)

Freed slaves fled westward from the Triangle, into the Hukaung Valley, a dreadful place destined for an invasion of strangers known as Merrill's Marauders.

In the Triangle the British set up a system of indirect rule. Local chiefs were allowed to keep their authority, but were subject to a *taung-ok*, a native overchief. To this position the British appointed Karui La Doi, a shrewd diplomat who knew and respected Kachin customs. With a handful of local police, he set up a headquarters at Kajihtu, where with remarkable success he maintained order and distributed justice.

The choice of La Doi turned out to be a fortunate one for Monsignor Usher. La Doi was in favor of having the Columbans start missions in his area, and the British saw it as a practical contribution to their plan for "Kachin regeneration."

Early in 1939 the monsignor sent Fathers James Stuart and Denis McAlindon into the Triangle to search for a suitable site for a new mission. They rode ponies north for twelve days, until provisions ran out. The Columbans had hoped to buy food along the way, but that was a year of rice famine. So on the long journey back to Myitkyina they subsisted on sweet potatoes and some fish and game.

In December, when the monsoon was past, Father Stuart, this time accompanied by Father James Doody, made another attempt to locate a site in the Triangle. The mission was still unaccomplished when they returned to Myitkyina for Christmas.

At the beginning of 1940 the two of them set off once more on the 165-mile trip. This time they were better equipped: four native helpers, four pack mules and enough food for several months.

From January to April they covered most of the south Triangle. They found it difficult making the chiefs understand that they were Irish, not English.

At Kajihtu they knew they had found the place. The gracious La Doi made them feel welcome. Father Stuart scouted for a site for the school and finally selected the summit of a hill above the village. La Doi assured him he would do his best to get the consent of the chief and village elders.

The Columbans hurried back to Myitkyina to tell the good news and to pack more provisions. As they started their return journey to Kajihtu the rains came. In the Triangle bridges wash out at the start of the monsoon, so the two priests had to take the long way around through Sumprabum.

After seemingly endless difficulties in getting themselves and their supplies across swollen rivers, they finally reached Kajihtu. There they settled down in a government bungalow to sit out the rain and to wait for La Doi to complete negotiations with the village elders for the property atop the hill.

In July Father Doody took ill and had to return to Myitkyina. This left Father Stuart alone for two months What a lonely time it was!

Finally the elders decided that the Columbans could have fifteen acres atop the hill. There at 3,500 feet above sea level, in an amphitheater formed by steep mountain ranges, the villagers began clearing the jungle. Father Stuart, his spirits up, started back to Myitkyina to tell the good news—new ground had been broken.

Monsignor Usher told Father Stuart that he was sending Father John Dunlea as a replacement for Father Doody. At the last moment, he decided to accompany them to Kajihtu and wrote home: "It is part of my work to go to see things myself. Then I understand them in terms of location, and energy expended, and I note the difficulties."

The trip started well but ended in a way no one had expected. The three

Columbans, riding along on their ponies, were aware that the jungle tangle concealed tigers and panthers and snakes. Yet the abundant wild life was mostly invisible. As an American soldier would write home four years later: "In the jungle what you see most is the noises."

The jungle, with all its thickets and tangle and profound shadows, is a frightening, chaotic place. It lacks the majestic grandeur of the forest. Forunately, much of the journey was through dense forests of teak trees, standing to tremendous heights to form a dark vault that blacks out the day.

Bad luck caught up with the travelers at Sumprabum. Although Kajihtu was only thirty-eight miles away, only three mule stages, two swollen rivers lay ahead.

During the delay the three Columbans put up at a dilapidated Kachin village. The people were friendly enough, and that was part of the problem: they insisted on serving food to their visitors.

Father Stuart, always one for needling, reminded his companions that the hill people ate snakes, frogs, field mice, and the pupae of various beetles. He had heard that Chins liked boiled dogs stuffed with a sweet, glutinous rice, and Karens considered cats a delicacy.

The monsignor responded to Father Stuart's needling by reminding him that in the Burmese language the words "delightful" and "diarrhea" sound much alike.

The missionaries sat in the doorway of a bamboo *basha* looking out on a dreary landscape. Inside the smoke and smells and gloom were unsettling. Besides, God's "little creatures" had inherited the place. Don't kill the lizards, Father Stuart told Father Dunlea, they eat the malaria-bearing mosquito. But do kill those things with so many legs; they carry a sting that brings agony for days.

The villagers came to visit the Columbans and talked and talked. One seemed exceptionally gossipy. Father Stuart nicknamed her "The Rangoon Gazette," and her daughter, "The Supplement."

"The Gazette" told of the night, a few months earlier, when "a frog ate the moon." The sight of an eclipse of the moon had so distressed three Indian bullock-cart drivers that they dumped on the ground the rice they were eating and used the pots and pans as cymbals to scare away the frog. When the moon continued to disappear the Indians sat beside the road and cried.

The gossipy woman described how village men had fired guns and women and children had beat on pots and pans to frighten the frog that was eating the moon. In time, as had always happened in the past, the frog disgorged its victim, and life returned to normal.

When the three priests continued their journey to Kajihtu, trouble rode with them. Inside them typhoid fever was incubating.

On his way back to Myitkyina Monsignor Usher developed a high fever but thought it was malaria. Up in Kajihtu, Fathers Stuart and Dunlea both took to their beds. The monsignor and Father Stuart recovered, but Father Dunlea died November 16, 1940.

The Kachins made a coffin of teakwood and every man, woman and child in the village attended the Requiem Mass. Afterward they buried John Dunlea atop a hill looking out toward the mountains of China and Tibet.

"It's a long way from Cork," James Stuart thought as Kachins filled in the grave.

Once more Father Stuart made the 165-mile journey back to Myitkyina. This time Monsignor Usher told him that his co-worker would be Father McAlindon. The two priests hurried to return to Kajihtu. They arrived on Christmas Eve.

Outside the village La Doi hurried to meet them. Behind him came all of the villagers. The priests and the people were no longer strangers; they had shared a universal experience. Each knew in the marrow that "It is appointed to man once to die."

·17·

War Reaches Burma

Just when Monsignor Usher thought that things were going well, war came to the Kachin hills. No one in Bhamo expected the Japanese to pour into southern Burma and race northward so fast.

"May 3, 1942, is a date we shall not easily forget," said the monsignor. At noon a distraught British doctor hurriedly returned from the front to report that Japanese soldiers were crossing the last bridge approaching Bhamo. He offered the monsignor and three other Columbans transportation to India. They thanked him saying they preferred to stay with their parishioners.

When the doctor asked them to take charge of the Bhamo Civil hospital, the monsignor agreed, wishing in his heart that the burden had not been thrust upon him. The place, in a state of chaos, housed many severe cases of smallpox. The priests soon discovered bodies that should have been buried days ago, for in Burma the dead must be interred within hours.

The Columbans felt forlorn as they watched civil administrators and military men in cars streaming out the north road. Shells made a fluttering sound passing over the hospital. The chatter of machine guns announced the Japanese entrance into Bhamo Town by the light of a brilliant moon.

The Japanese commander asked time and again, "Why didn't you leave for India?" The answer was always, "Our place is with our parishioners."

The Irish priests tried to explain their position of neutrality, but the Japanese commander said, "English, Irish, all same."

The commander decided to put the Columbans under "Protective Custody" in Bhamo jail. He had a way of saying "Protective Custody" that put the sound of a capital letter at the beginning of each word.

Columbans were brought in from their remote parishes in the hills. Each arrived at the flea-infested Bhamo jail with a story to tell. For instance, Father Doody was accused of being a spy. The Japanese tried to persuade him to admit it, and when he would not they tied him up and beat him. That continued for a couple of days before they threatened to kill him. At the first opportunity he escaped into the jungle. After a day he was recaptured and given a few more beatings on the way to Bhamo jail.

On June 18, 1942, the Columbans were released from jail to find the town a scene of desolation. The church was in a filthy state; their house and school had been burned.

On the sixth anniversary of the monsignor's arrival in Burma, October 28, hopes ran high. From Tokyo, in response to a request from the Vatican, came an order that the missionaries should be protected.

The commander in Bhamo ordered all Columbans to start for Mandalay immediately. He probably wanted to be free of the responsibility, or may even have thought that he was being helpful. As it turned out he was doing them no favor.

They had to pay their own way for their journey into captivity. To make things worse they were assigned to an unsafe riverboat; the nineteen priests and six native helpers had to exist in a deck space of eighteen by twelve feet. No one was permitted to turn in his sleep or lie on his back for there was not enough room. To remain in one position was especially penitential because of the rivets in the sheet-metal deck. Rain poured down most of the time in the twelve days down the Irrawaddy from Bhamo to Mandalay, a trip that should have taken at most three or four days.

As the boat approached the dock at Mandalay, the priests came upon a scene of such desolation that they flinched at the sight of it. They remembered the Mandalay of a few years earlier, and now all was chaotic rubble as far as the horizon. No city was ever more thoroughly burned.

From the river the Columbans made a cheerless trek to a house that belonged to the Mandalay Agricultural College well outside the city. What a luxury, to lie on a wooden floor and stretch and turn at will—after that sheet-metal deck.

Some of the Columbans were still on the run having been able to evade the Japanese so far. As said in an earlier chapter, Fathers Stuart and Mc-Alindon were still in the Triangle, up in Kajihtu, but would soon become legends all over Burma.

Fathers William Kehoe and Michael Kelly were the first to feel pressure from the invading army, but the Japanese never caught them. Sometimes the two young priests wondered if life might have been more pleasant as prisoners of war.

Monsignor Usher was worried about those two missionaries down in

Kengtung, sixty miles from the French IndoChina border. As soon as the Japanese entered Burma, right after Pearl Harbor, he ordered Fathers Kehoe and Kelly back to Bhamo. "It is your duty," he wrote, "and you have no choice."

But it was too late. They spent months on the run. Burying the dead, avoiding tigers, fearing the head-hunting Wars. Their lives for the next two years would make a book full of nightmares. Finally, they reached Kunming, China, and were flown across the Himalayas to Assam, where they were held in detention for several days until British intelligence could clear them of any suspicion of spy activity.

Eventually, they were assigned parishes in India—Father Kelly in Calcutta and Father Kehoe in New Delhi, where our paths must have crossed many times.

During the early days of war, two other Columbans, Fathers Jeremiah Kelleher and James Cloonan, were becoming heroes.

Father Kelleher would have shared the Bhamo jail with his confreres had he not volunteered to go southward with a unit of Kachin soldiers. Down in the war zone the British made him a military chaplain.

When Rangoon fell, March 8, 1942, a battalion of the Enniskilling fusiliers was flown into Magwe. Chaplain Kelleher hurried to join the Irish soldiers, who moved dierectly to Prome. The unit is about sixty percent Catholic, said Colonel Cox, of Belfast, upon welcoming the chaplain most graciously.

The British were fighting a losing battle. As the Japanese moved into one side of Prome the British troops fled out the other.

Many times Father Kelleher was near death. Once, while traveling in a truck, men on each side of him were killed by machine-gun bullets. On another occasion when he was left near dead behind enemy lines, a young officer slipped through and brought him out.

A soldier from Tralee, while convalescing, wrote of Chaplain Kelleher: "He was generally to be found, when not attending the wounded, in the front line with the men fighting the rearguard action. He was in turn priest, stretcher-bearer, nurse and doctor. He comforted the living and buried the dead, so much so that, dressed in rags and shaking with fever, when he reached Myitkyina the doctor pronounced him unfit to travel any farther."

The convalescing soldier was impressed that the chaplain refused a chance to go to India. There he would have been safe from the war. Instead he decided to stay at Myitkyina to help the refugees and the wounded.

Father Cloonan also preferred to stay in Myitkyina; he refused to fly by air transport to India.

An Australian Redemptorist wrote of his admiration for Father Cloonan: "A real hero, if ever there was one. I owe him a deep debt of gratitude. . . . Such utter selfless devotion, especially in one far from being physically robust, surely deserves the name of heroism. To work twenty hours a day, with never a thought for himself and the smile never fading from his eyes, was heroism of a pretty high order if I know anything about it."

When the Japanese reached Myitkyina on May 9 they arrested Fathers Kelleher and Cloonan. The two Columbans were held in the Baptist mission compound for three months before being sent south to Rangoon. There they were under strict house arrest for the three remaining years of war.

Meanwhile in Mandalay the Columbans were being held in a house surrounded by Japanese units, and, of course, that attracted the attention of Allied bombers. Drums of gasoline stored all about did not contribute to peace of mind, as day after day and night after night, the prisoners endured air raids.

The Japanese kept the Columbans in custody but would not feed them and would not even consider selling them rice at controlled prices. Fortunately, Monsignor Usher had 10,000 rupees.

Suddenly, the Japanese said they wanted to occupy the house and that the Columbans would have to move to Saint John's Leper Asylum. When the missionaries moved in with 300 lepers they thought that at last they would be free from air raids, but not so. In one twenty-four hour period they absorbed thirteen raids. The place was nearly destroyed by a lone bomber on a pitch black night. Somehow Major Brown of the U.S. Air Corps learned about the prisoners in the asylum and he and a former Baptist missionary, Captain Cummings, passed the word along to the pilots, and from that day on no bombs fell within a mile of the leper colony.

The internees kept their sanity by keeping busy. They repaired clothing, baked bread and made shoes. They gathered and cut firewood, cared for pigs and a cow and planted a gigantic garden.

Monsignor Usher wrote the history of the Catholic Church in Burma, and Father Way prepared a catechism for children and one for adults and learned to read music and play the organ.

The most nerve-racking days came as the war drew to a close. When the British were moving in to recapture Mandalay, the Japanese placed a big gun in front of the leper asylum and, of course, the British fired back.

The strain began to tell. Everyone became visibly more gaunt. Day or night there was hardly a moment free from the sound of shells and machine guns, mortars and hand grenades.

On the morning of March 16, 1945, a stray Japanese shell burst above the room used as a chapel, tore the top off the tabernacle, pierced the Mass book and penetrated the altar table. Of the twelve priests in the room, several were wounded but none so severely as Father Thomas Murphy. One foot was mangled and there was a severe wound in his stomach.

Father McEvoy volunteered to go for help. He slipped out the back and waded through a canal to reach a British outpost. The officer in charge sent a radio message to headquarters for help; headquarters promised that if necessary they would fly Father Murphy to India within two hours.

Father Murphy seemed to know it was the end. He said good-bye, begged pardon for his faults and promised to keep the Columbans in his prayers.

To save time the stretcher-bearers decided to use the main road. The Japanese held their fire and the group arrived safely at the British outpost. But before the ambulance could reach the field hospital Father Murphy was dead.

When the stretcher-bearers returned, they brought news that the British would send trucks for any prisoner who could reach an assembly point three miles away. The trucks could not come closer because they would be shelled by the Japanese.

The missionaries and other internees, about 160 in all, slipped out the back way, sloshed through a canal and moved along a remote road in uneasy procession—a nun with a broken leg, several patients so weakened by fever they had to be carried, and a few priests hobbling along with pieces of shrapnel in their legs. On his back Father Edmund McGovern carried a French bishop, age eighty. In spite of all the pain, they moved with spirit. Had it not been for Father Murphy's death it would have been a glorious Saint Patrick's Day.

·18·

But Not Weeping

Monsignor Usher wrote home: "Among the ashes of our buildings we sit, but not weeping."

It was probably his first day back in Bhamo, there among the ashes, that I saw him loom in the door. That "look of eagles," alert and intense, so embedded itself in my memory that thirty years later I recognized his photograph in the archives in Killiney.

The Columbans were shocked when they returned to Bhamo. Scarcely a house was standing. Everywhere were trenches, shell holes and bomb craters. In Myitkyina and Katha all buildings were gone. And so it was in Meinhkat, Hpunpyen and Zaubung.

The Columbans sat down amid the ashes and wrote home letters of good feeling. As Monsignor Usher said: "The priests are overjoyed with the steadiness of the Catholics during our separation from them. With comparatively few defectors we find the main body with a more lively faith than when last we saw them."

Monsignor Usher was still impatient to be up and doing, and yet war had taught him something about mortality and its limitations. "You must be content with a very limited degree of success in your lifetime," he wrote. "Be satisfied with the less congenial work of clearing the ground and winning from it the first thin returns. For the later workers is reserved the happier task of gathering the rich harvest."

Whether or not he was aware of it, this was the attitude of his patron, the great Patrick. The Saint, so it is said, accepted both the gains and losses of life with equal gratitude because of his unshaken hope in the promises of Providence.

Monsignor Usher returned to Ireland for a holiday and soon found himself homesick for the missions. Upon returning to Bhamo he wrote to a priest back home: "What I was not prepared for was the leap up of the heart when I saw old Burma again. I am still astonished at it, and enormously happy about it." He admitted that his bones were tired after so much journeying, but gave assurance that he would not change places with any man, woman or child in the world. "I tell you it is worth enduring a holiday for the joy of coming back."

Several thousand people gathered for three days in Bhamo, in March of 1949, to honor Patrick Usher on his twenty-five years as a priest. It seemed an unending stream, visitors pouring into the mission compound by foot, pony, truck, jeep and bullock cart. The Kachin hill people were in the majority; their gowns mixed red and silver into the crowd and their turbans added touches of white and yellow. The Shans brought blue to the assembly and the Burmese a blaze of many colors. There were also Australians, New Zealanders, Spaniards, Irishmen, Chinese, British, Italians, Bengalis and Gurkhas.

When the Monsignor addressed the vast assembly he spoke of the schools the Columbans had started and those they hope to start. Nothing the monsignor might say would more enlarge their affection for the Columbans. Ever since the war they had been especially hungry for education, having seen things that they wanted for themselves, or a least for their children.

They had noticed that even the lowest GI, when on a rest break, might lean against a banyan tree and begin to read. (The military published thirty well-known books each month in editions shaped to fit the pocket of a combat jacket.) They had observed that no sooner did the U.S. Army take a town than it began a daily mimeographed newspaper to keep the soldiers informed.

The Kachins and Shans were astonished, and so was I, at how soon the Americans established a radio station whenever the gunfire died down. While writing in my deserted Buddhist monastery I used to hear the disk jockey say, "Coming to you from beautiful downtown Bhamo!" All through the hills the tribesmen listened to "Praise the Lord and Pass the Ammunition" and "Don't Sit Under the Apple Tree with Anyone Else but Me."

Within a decade after Patrick Usher's speech, Kachins from Columban schools were enrolled at Rangoon University. The missionaries had forty-seven primary schools, six middle schools and four high schools.

The health of the tribesmen was something else with which the Columbans concerned themselves. The monsignor instructed the missionaries to open dispensaries as soon as possible and to pray for the day when they could afford clinics.

Anyone operating a dispensary in Burma soon came to realize that nature in those hills is not benign. Monsoons, insects, snakes, elephants and tigers all had a way of disrupting physical well-being.

All was going well except for Patrick Usher's health. He was even beginning to talk about taking a rest in Ireland. He wrote to a friend: "For a year or two back I have been talking about 1959 as the year I would go home. Now it is fixed. I have asked for a leave of absence from March 15 to October 15, that is to say for all the year that is worth having."

He wanted to return to County Louth, where he had been born at Tully-allen, May 12, 1899, and see once more Ireland's hawthorne hedgerows in May. Of course he would have to be back in Burma in time to be consecrated as the first bishop of the Diocese of Bhamo. The ceremony was to be held at Christmas in 1959 in the new Saint Patrick's Cathedral that was being built even as he lay dying.

He was "not in good form," as the Irish say, throughout the summer of 1958. He suffered pains in his left shoulder and arm, the side that would eventually become paralyzed.

Patrick Usher died Monday, October 13, 1958. Chinese carpenters made the coffin with care. Masons working on the new cathedral paused to line the grave with brick and cover it with concrete.

Beneath a scorching sun, thousands of mourners, of many creeds, walked the two miles to the Bhamo Christian cemetery, reciting the rosary in many languages along the way. One of the twenty-one priests present said, "Certainly he did not appear before God with empty hands."

Chaplain Harold Henry with Bishop Germain Mousset in Seoul, Korea

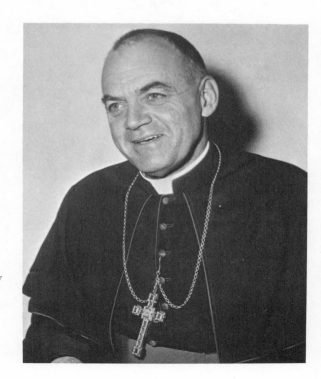

Archbishop Harold Henry
of Kwangju, Korea

Archbishop Henry's funeral on Cheju Island, Korea

Father Patrick McGlinchey's farm on Cheju Island

One of Father McGlinchey's prize pigs

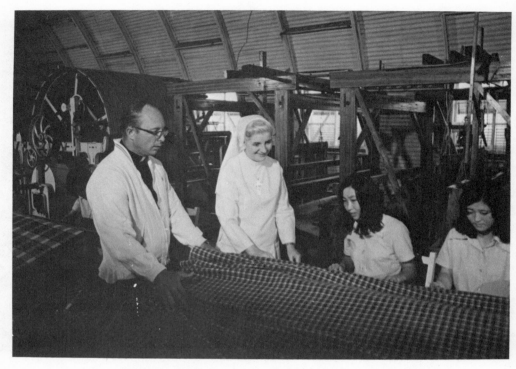

Father Frank Roger, Sister M. Rosarii, and weavers on Cheju Island

Columban Sisters' Hospital in Mokpo, Korea

Sister Enda Stanton, M.D., at Mokpo church picnic

Archbishop Patrick Gronin of Mindanao, the Philippines

The legendary Father Patrick Stuart of Burma

Monsignor Patrick Usher in Bhamo, Burma

Father Bernard Way and a Kachin family

Bishop John Howe and his successor, Bishop Paul Grawng

Father Martin Dobey and Fijian boys

Archbishop Petero Mataca on a pilgrimage of reconciliation in Fiji

Frances Lewis (Mother Mary Patrick, cofounder of the Missionary Sisters of St. Columban) on her engagement to Sir Alfred Moloney

Bishop Edward Galvin, cofounder of the Society of St. Columban, in Hanyang, China

Father Cornelius Tierney (*above*) and Father Timothy Leonard (*below*) died violent deaths in China. They were among the first of twenty Columbans to die for their faith.

Father Kevin Flynn, the author's
invaluable guide to Japan

Brother Zeno of Japan

Brother Zeno with retarded children

·19·

The New Bishop

When Patrick Usher died Father John Howe was assigned as his replacement. The young priest had been doing remarkable work, since the end of the war, up in remote Tanghpre.

When Father Howe arrived in Tanghpre, in July of 1945, he began building a rude presbytery, a chapel and a boarding school. Although the three structures of bamboo and thatch were, in the beginning, no more substantial than baskets, they stood in a lovely place, the dramatic spot where two rivers coming down from the Himalayas join to form the Irrawaddy.

Starting with this compound as a center Father Howe worked to establish a Christian village. He found the virgin soil excellent for farming, especially since it is enriched by silt from the Irrawaddy. He solved one irrigation problem with pipe the military had used to get oil along the Ledo Road from Burma to China. As for working the soil, he dreamed of dispensing with bullocks in favor of tractor-drawn ploughs. A sawmill was also high on his list of dreams.

Tanghpre, so nicely set in a ring of hills, seemed an ideal place to develop a mission compound. Many Kachins from the wilderness of the north could not help but become aware of it because they use the paths through there and stop at the confluence to rest on their way to Myitkyina. Their backs bent under loads of vegetables, fruit and sesame seed, they plod down to the bazaar thirty miles south. After trading for salt, rice, thread and cloth, they make the long trek back under especially heavy loads. So it has been for centuries.

There was one problem—Tanghpre was not healthy; no school should be built there. In prewar days that would have been the death of a dream, but in 1945 John Howe knew exactly what an efficient U.S. Army insecticide team could do. With the help of his army friends the area was made safe.

In time there were forty families in the village where there had been only five. Each made a tidy living cultivating the earth that a few years earlier had been under a mantle of semitropical jungle. The Catholic commmunity that Father Howe had envisioned had become a reality. Benediction of the Blessed Sacrament, May Devotions, Stations of the Cross and even an annual retreat became a normal part of life. In a district where formerly there was not a Catholic, Tanghpre became the center and inspiration of a parish of 500. From the three Columban schools in the area many of the students went on to attend St. Columban's High School in Myitkyina.

John Howe pushed to completion the cathedral that Patrick Usher had planned. He set the dedication ceremony for March 14, 1961, observing that the year was an appropriate one for dedicating a cathedral to Saint Patrick since it was the 1,500th centenary of the Saint's death. Fifteen thousand Christians, Hindus, Mohammedans and Buddhists attended the festivities that began on Tuesday and continued until Thursday. Although the occasion was in the main religious, there was a feast that used 450 bushels of rice, a gift from U Nu, prime minister of the Union of Burma.

Within a month of the dedication of Saint Patrick's, word reached Burma that Pope John XXIII was raising the prefecture of Bhamo to a diocese that would stretch from just north of Mandalay to Tibet.

When John Howe became a bishop on July 1, 1961, the ceremony took place in Saint Patrick's, at Bhamo. The archbishop of Rangoon was present along with two Columban bishops, Harold Henry from Korea and Patrick Cronin from Mindanao.

The consecrating prelate, the archbishop of Mandalay, was assisted by the bishops of Bassein and Toungoo. Bishop Howe was pleased that the three consecrators were the first members of the Burma hierarchy to come from the ranks of local clergy. By now he knew that the years of the Columbans in Burma were numbered and that the time was coming when all foreigners would have to leave.

In his first report as bishop he stressed the need to educate for the religious life more young people native to Burma. The supply of priests, Sisters and Brothers from abroad could no longer be depended on. He knew that several priests and nuns were standing by in the United States and Ireland waiting to make the trip—their superiors had told him so—but foreigners were not being granted entrance visas. The government of Burma was beginning to close the door.

His report, in 1961, was still optimistic. He recalled that Patrick Usher had arrived twenty-five years earlier to find only 3,000 Catholics in upper Burma, and now there were 28,000.

Bishop Howe very much wanted to establish a medical clinic. That he would get one seemed improbable because the government was not allowing foreigners to enter Burma. But then, quite providentially, the government allowed several Columban Sisters with medical training to enter.

The location of the clinic, on the Ledo Road sixty-five miles from Myitkyina, was "a beautiful scenic spot," a Columban Sister recalls. "At night tigers peered at us in the dark. Monkeys, with their not-too-melodious chatter, awakened us each morning."

No sooner had the Sisters arrived, in October of 1963, than they began to dream of a mobile clinic, one that might operate up and down the length of the Ledo Road. These hopes were never realized, though, because when the Burmese and the Kachins began to war with each other, the Sisters were caught in the crossfire.

Perhaps the highlight of Bishop Howe's time in Burma was when he ordained Paul Grawng the first Kachin priest. He little dreamed that eleven years later, April 3, 1976, he would ordain him the first Kachin bishop.

Paul Grawng has what the Kachin's call *myit su ai*—prudence, wisdom, dignity. He would need all such virtues, Bishop Howe thought, because he will soon carry the burden as leader of the Catholic Church in upper Burma.

War and rebellion plagued many parts of the country after Burma achieved independence from the British in 1948. When the Kachins sought complete independence from the Union of Burma, life became most difficult for the Columbans. Since their parishioners were mainly Kachins, they made a special point of not becoming political. The missionaries were so faithful to this policy that no one ever accused them of interfering. They had come to preach the gospel and that is what they did.

The government was not against them as Christians but did disapprove of them as a foreign influence. A decree in 1962 stated that if foreign missionaries left the country for any reason whatever they would not be given reentry visas. This meant that the old hands stayed on and on and their health declined with the years.

The last three Columbans departed Rangoon in July of 1979. They left behind eight confreres who had died in Burma.

·20·

Burma Remembered

As I interviewed the Columbans, much of what they said brought back my days in Burma. When they spoke of the "big three" of snakedom —cobras, kraits and Russell's vipers—I remembered two incidents from the spring of 1945.

A war correspondent, holding a small, limp snake high in the air, came into the Buddhist monastery where I was writing, and said, "I just saw this outside the door and gave it a good whacking." He did not know that what he had killed was a krait, the most deadly snake in that part of the world.

A few evenings later I stepped outside the monastery door where two lines of statues of the Buddha faced each other down the length of a courtyard. A dense tangle of vines covered much of the ground, for the jungle was beginning to reclaim the place. American soldiers had set up a hoop in the courtyard and were shooting baskets. A tired sergeant began to sit down in a tangle of vines. I said, "Be careful, sergeant, a cobra lives there!" Not realizing that I was merely joking, he paused, and in that moment a cobra slithered out and glided the length of the court between the great stone statues.

When missionaries spoke of rats, I again remembered Bhamo. How defiant the rats were! I would throw heavy combat boots at them, across the room, but they would merely duck to one side and hold their ground. At night I made sure the netting was tucked in around the edge of the bed, not only to keep out malaria-bearing mosquitos, but also to hinder arrogant rats.

The Columbans were rat-conscious because rodents carried fleas that brought the bubonic plague to Bhamo. When the Bhamo bazaar caught fire, in 1939, rats jumped onto food trucks and soon delivered their plague fleas all over the area. When the rats began dropping dead by the hundreds, villagers began dying, too. Rat hunts were formed in village after village. While some men pried up floor boards, others clubbed rats as they jumped out. A normal catch was from 150 to 200 rats a house.

When the Columbans spoke of rogue elephants and man-eating tigers, my memories went back to my early days in Myitkyina. At night, from my tent in a jungle clearing, I listened to the trumpeting of bull elephants across the Irrawaddy. One night when I posted guards to watch for infiltrating Japanese, one guard gave away his position by firing at a tiger that had come down to the Irrawaddy for a drink. Up the Ledo Road a tiger ripped the side out of a bamboo basha and scalped a soldier inside; the victim grabbed an automatic rifle and shot the attacker full of holes.

Father William Kehoe was right that day in Killiney when he observed that of all the places in the world the United States Army could have sent me it was providential that my assignments had been to Myitkyina and Bhamo. Living there in a remote section of Burma gave me the feeling that I needed to write the book.

When writing about Father Stuart, in an earlier chapter, I said that I had been sent to Burma to run mule trains through the jungle. That story begins in the spring of 1944 at Fort Benning, Georgia, where I was writing training manuals at the Infantry School. A notice appeared on the bulletin board asking for volunteers to organize Animal Pack Transportation Units. Mule trains.

Mules were carrying supplies across mountains and through jungles of upper Burma where Merrill's Marauders fought the Japanese. The Marauders, all volunteers, made it possible to build the Ledo Road from India, across Burma, to China.

The Army accepted my willingness to study the mystery of mules, maybe because I had grown up on a farm in Kentucky. Anyway, I spent four weeks at the Cavalry School, at Fort Riley, Kansas, along with cowboys, horse trainers, polo players, ranchers and jockeys.

We learned to throw single diamond, double diamond and squaw hitches. We studied shoeing, spavins and saddle sores, matters that are not normal concerns of the day.

A journey began from Fort Riley that ended on the other side of the world on Christmas Eve. Three days by train from Kansas to California. Two weeks of waiting at the port of embarkation. Thirty days by ship to Bombay. Eight by train across India to Assam. Three down the Ledo Road by truck. And now the last stop on the Irrawaddy River, near Myitkyina.

Upon entering the clearing at dusk I was surprised to hear Bing Crosby's voice singing, "Silent Night." The gramophone looked out of place there on the ammunition box in front of a tent. I entered the tent and handed my orders to a disheveled major who reeked of bourbon. He squinted at the dimly printed mimeographed sheet, held it nearer the candle, and read it with moving lips. His face went a little off-center while he paused, deciding how best to say it.

"Lieutenant, we don't really need you."

Christmas Eve. On the other side of the world. And they don't need me!

"We don't use mule trains any more. We air drop. Fly in low and kick the stuff out by parachute."

As I left the major's tent, "Silent Night" played on. I had not noticed the crack in the record: thump . . . thump . . . thump.

I never realized that the Columban influence was entering my consciousness on that, one of the darkest nights of my life. Crosby had recorded "Silent Night" as a favor for a Columban missionary.

Father Richard Ranaghan, returning from Hanyang in the mid-1930s, brought home some film footage showing missionaries at work in China. When he stopped at Paramount Studios to have a sound track added, Crosby sang "Silent Night" over a Christmas sequence. Up until then Bing had always felt that "sacred songs were a little out of my league." The record became one of the best sellers of all time.

Within a few days I was assigned to escort fifty-seven war correspondents on the first convoy across the Ledo-Burma Road. Upon finishing the thousand-mile journey at Kunming, China, I flew the Hump across the Himalayas to Myitkyina only to learn that the military headquarters had moved to Bhamo. So I flew down there and was told to write the military history of upper Burma.

When the manuscript about the missionaries, called *Mission in Burma*, was complete in September of 1979, I took it to the Columbans' seminary at Navan, in County Meath, where several old Burma hands would read it. As I was packing the manuscript, getting ready for the trip, a radio newscast told about Lord Louis Mountbatten's funeral that day; he had been killed in Ireland a week earlier.

This, too, brought back memories of Bhamo. Mountbatten, the supreme Allied commander in Southeast Asia, had given me my most pleasant week of the war. He sent a radio message to Bhamo asking that I come to his headquarters at Kandy, Ceylon.

While I was sitting at the edge of a long, empty field waiting for a plane, Father Stuart came along and asked if he might hitch a ride to one of our intermediary stops. As we sat in the hot glare of the sun he spoke about the Columban missionaries, the only time I ever heard him talk about the work that had brought him to Burma. He and I would both have been surprised to know that the things he spoke of would, in time, occupy the sixth decade of my life.

Mountbatten was surprised at how fast the U.S. pilots got me to Kandy. He said, "I did not expect you for another week." So he assigned me a car and a chauffeur and suggested I spend several days seeing Ceylon. Eventually, at lunch he said that since I was writing a history for the United States Army I might well give him a copy and then he would not have to assign someone to cover the same material.

When I landed at Dublin, the day after Mountbatten's funeral, Father McGonagle, an old Burma hand, drove me to Navan. There he settled me into a suite—bedroom, bath and study—usually reserved for bishops. He called my attention to the Hill of Tara, framed in the windows of bedroom and study.

When I expressed delight at the view, a Columban took me on a walk up to Tara where the high kings of Ireland held forth 1,500 years ago and where Saint Patrick is said to have visited. Tourists, having heard of the harp that played in Tara's halls, came to the spot and find that sheep now graze where the harp once played.

The next day jet lag hit me hard as it always does. When my inner clocks are thrown out of synch I feel washed-out, letdown and depressed. That has been the bane of all my travels.

I had to pull myself together, though, because in midmorning Bishop Howe and Fathers Kelleher, Cloonan and Foley came to my study to talk about how best to handle the review of the Burma manuscript. I said they ought each to read it and make notes and then meet together to discuss their observations.

Even though I felt dreary that morning I wrote in my journal: "What remarkable men the old Burma hands are! They have a certain inner light that is warm and good. When Father Steinhilber was superior general he told me that in visiting missionaries all over the world he found the spirit of the priests in Burma the most admirable. He marveled at how they treated one another with such deference and kindness. Of all the Columban missions why was that of Burma the most spiritual?"

I took all of my meals at the seminary with retired missionaries. They had wonderful stories to tell, having lived under unusual conditions all over the world. Some have been held for ransom by bandits; most have been near death time and again.

One day at lunch Father McGonagle asked if I had ridden elephants in Burma. No, I said, but I did in India. While visiting the Maharajah of Jaipur he turned me over to his chief huntsman to take me on what he called "a tiger shoot." We traveled by way of elephant.

It was evident that Father McGonagle felt the elephants I had associated with were much too domesticated. He seemed interested in the rogues.

"If an elephant attacks," he said, "try to find a hill to run down and run in a zig-zag pattern. That's because the elephant touches the ground with his trunk before putting down his foot on that spot; in going down hill it is harder for him to touch earth with his trunk. On a straight run he can catch you because he works up to a speed of forty miles an hour. Another defense is to climb a tree so thick that he cannot uproot it, or shake you out of it."

He said that when a mahout is leading an elephant past something dangerous he turns the beast's head toward the danger. The animal feels more comfortable keeping an eye on the danger.

The old missionary told with admiration of the delicate manipulations an elephant performs with his trunk: "He pulls a branch from a tree, plucks off most leaves while holding it down with his foot, keeps a few leaves on the end and then switches it over his shoulder to shoo away whatever is annoying him."

I asked if an elephant really does have a long memory. "I would say they do," said Father McGonagle, "Oh, yes, I would say so. If a mahout mistreats an elephant, sooner or later the beast will kill him. They really do remember, yes they do."

While waiting for the Burma manuscript to be checked I walked around the seminary grounds for several hours each day. During frequent stops at the cemetery I was reminded of what a poor longevity record the Columbans have. Marble tablets list the nearly 300 who have died since the Society started in 1918. Not one had lived to be ninety, as of that September in 1979. Two had reached eighty-nine. Many died young. The average longevity was probably, at best, forty-five. I have seen enough of life on the missions to understand why.

Bishop Howe returned the manuscript of *Mission in Burma* to me after he and Fathers Kelleher, Kehoe and Foley had spent sixteen days going through it. Here and there they corrected a date and the spelling of names, but the only substantial change was in the two final chapters. They made more diplomatic some statements about the government of Burma. Bishop Howe explained that they did not want the Kachin priests to suffer because of any harsh remarks.

All of the old Burma hands spoke with enthusiasm about the manuscript. They found delight in it because it brought back so many poignant memories: musical laughter down a village street at dusk; the throb of temple bells; silence in the teak forests; clouds of green parrots over the river; white herons standing gaunt in a rice paddy and, ah, the scent of jasmine.

I spoke of their homesickness to Father Kehoe and he said: "The homesickness will wear away in time. Ah, yes, I'd say it will. Time heals, some."

·21·

The Ways of Fiji

The longer I am around Columbans the more I admire their anecdotes. Theirs is an oral tradition. But experiences passed along by word of mouth tend to die out. Once lost they are as irretrievable as yesterday.

I used to think about this while walking in the cemetery at Navan. What stories the dead might tell: tigers along the Irrawaddy, Japanese snipers in Mindanao, starvation in Korea, floods along the Yangtze, ashes in Nagasaki.

The more I read the names of the stones the more I wanted to get the anecdotes down on paper before it was too late. Upon leaving the cemetery in such a mood, one afternoon in September of 1979, I came upon Father Martin Dobey.

He was mowing the lawn in front of the seminary building. When I introduced myself, he said that he was on holiday but felt the need for exercise.

I asked where he had been stationed and he said Fiji. Twenty-seven years. He would not be returning; he had a new assignment in Australia.

He spoke of the islands and the Fijians with such affection that I felt his story ought to be told. And so I said that if he would meet me in Fiji a year hence, and if he showed me around the islands, I would write a book about the people and their ways. Although I had not given this thought, and knew nothing about Fiji, I did not hesitate to make the offer because it had the feeling of rightness about it, the thing to be aware of in making any large decision, for that is the area of the providential.

Martin Dobey said that after his ordination, at Christmas of 1950, he and his classmates had continued their studies at Navan. With mounting expectation they awaited their assignments.

Over and over they reviewed the possibilities: China seemed an improbable place to go now that the Communists were in power; the situation there was most unstable. Maybe the Philippines. Or Korea. Or Japan. Martin Dobey preferred Burma, but there, too, the government was beginning to close the door.

At Easter the announcement came: Fiji!

In all of their seminary days they had not heard the word. The announcement said that the Columbans had accepted an invitation from the bishop of Fiji. Thirteen would soon leave for the islands.

When a launch pulled alongside their steamer, February 22, 1952, an agile man sprang aboard and introduced himself as Bishop Victor Foley. With him were five husky Fijian warriors, of formidable features, displaying well-oiled chests, leaf skirts of bark cloth, and an explosion of dense, fuzzy hair.

The chief began a ceremony, the Raising of the Anchor, one that dates back to the days when no chief dared land in another's district without permission. Through an interpreter the missionaries learned that they were receiving permission.

The chief presented the priests with four whale teeth. No amount of money or political pressure can win a whale's tooth, the highest honor a Fijian can bestow. The award is given to those believed to be worthy of it.

During a ceremony at the cathedral that evening, the Fijians gave the priests five more whale teeth. As part of the ceremony the hosts prepared *yagona*, sometimes called *kava*, and it was then the foreigners realized that they were in a land of exacting ceremony, and that they had better learn the traditions, and learn them well.

On my first night in Fiji I, too, was impressed with the power of tradition. When Father Dobey met me at the Nadi airport, August 19, 1980, he said we would be attending a ceremony that evening, not one to welcome me but to say good-bye to an Australian family.

Right off I felt awkward and embarrassed, as always, when introduced to a culture foreign to me. In trying to take part in an unfamiliar ceremony or alien custom there comes an uneasy sense of artificiality, almost the guilty feeling of dishonesty. Such hauntings were there at the farewell party for Dr. Basil McNamara, his wife Patricia and their two children. Dr. McNamara, a surgeon in Fiji for five years, would soon be moving to a clinic in his native Australia.

The party was under a tent surrounded by banana and frangipani trees. Upon entering the private garden, the hundred guests removed their shoes and sat cross-legged on the mat of pandanus leaves. From infants to ancients they represented a cross section of the population—Fijians, Indians, Tongans, Rotumans, Europeans and many racial blendings.

A *kava* ceremony, a solemn one, started the evening. A gigantic man, who in spite of great bulk could sit with feet tucked beneath himself, spoke at length and with feeling. A more delicate Fijian strained a muddy liquid through the tough strands of fiber pulled from the dried bark of the wild hibiscus plant.

Kava is to Fiji what tea is to England and beer to Germany, only more so. In the old days it was prepared by having virginal girls with strong teeth chew a piece of pepper plant root and spit it into a wooden tub; to this was added water and the mixture strained through the husk of a coconut. The government now prohibits this method, and so the roots are pulverized by a more hygenic means. The drink, nonalcholic, is believed to be a tranquilizer, calming tempers when discussions become heated.

The bulky man held a coconut shell of *kava* in both hands and extended it, with outstretched arms, to Dr. McNamara. Before accepting it, the surgeon brought his cupped hands together in three claps, a requirement, and drained the cup at one gulp, also according to custom. Patricia and Father Dobey clapped and drained their cups.

My time was at hand. Father Dobey introduced me as "a professor from a distinguished university, known as Notre Dame." The clapping would be easy but the single gulp would take will power. It went down with a "green" taste and a tingling sensation.

I asked Dr. MacNamara what ailments in Fiji take up most of his time. Bleeding ulcers are common, he said.

I expressed surprise: The Fijians have a reputation for being so relaxed.

"The things that bother them are not the same that bother us," said the surgeon. "They get paid today; they spend the money today, and they do not worry about tomorrow. They also have no sense of time. If a Fijian is to meet another at six o'clock today but does not show up until six o'clock tomorrow, it does not bother either of them. That would bother us.

"However, slights and imagined slights gnaw at them. This *kava* ceremony is important to them. We can't imagine how important. If you gave a cocktail party and somebody failed to come, or failed to drink with you, it would not gnaw at you. A Fijian might see it as a great slight."

This increased my uneasiness. Would some awkwardness in dealing with their culture be seen as a great slight and gnaw at the Fijian soul? To lessen my chances of acting like a lout I took a book about Fijian customs to bed and tried to memorize it beneath the mosquito netting.

Despite the midnight cramming I felt unprepared for the test when we left the next morning for the village of Votua. I still rehearsed the warnings: Do not have hands in pockets, or talk loudly, or whistle or sing when walking through the village. Don't carry a towel or bag on shoulder, but in the hand. Do not walk side by side or wear a hat. "All of this," explained the book, "is to show respect and honor to the people of the village."

I hoped we would play tourists and look at the village from the truck, but in my heart I knew that as soon as Father Dobey appeared people would crowd around and insist that we visit someone's home. And that is what happened.

We walked down the village street, surrounded by an ever-gathering crowd, past houses with thatched roofs and reed walls, most with a compact, well-designed look. A few, though, were like scruffy haystacks.

We turned toward the front door of one of the better houses with the canons of courtesy echoing in my mind: "Always remove shoes and socks before entering the house. Do not remove them while standing on the threshold. The threshold (*i lago*) has a very special significance and should not be stepped on, or sat on, or anything done to it."

I removed shoes and was careful about the threshold.

"It is not courteous to stand inside a house. One should sit down immediately on entering." And so we did.

"While sitting two postures are permissible—sitting cross-legged or sitting with legs outstretched. It is not courteous to sit with knees tucked up to one's chin." It was while sitting with legs outstretched that I noticed I had forgotten to take off my socks. Take them off now, or leave them on? Let them stay!

If one wishes to stretch one's legs, says the book, it is courteous to ask permission by saying, "*au dodo yava mada*," or *au via dodo*," or "*au sa dodo*," or "*au sa dodo mada*." Better to endure cramped muscles than attempt asking permission to stretch, I thought.

"While moving inside, walk stooped or better, crawl on one's knees," the book had advised. "Be careful not to walk behind seated people; on entering or leaving always walk in front, bowing as you go, with right hand and palm outstretched—the symbol and sign of openness and courtesy." Others walked around the room bowed almost double, but I stayed put.

While Father Dobey carried on an animated conversation in Fijian, I reviewed the courtesy catechism: Do not stand with hands on hips. Do not touch a Fijian person on the head. The custom of men holding hands does not have the overtones it has in some other cultures.

Finally, Father Dobey said to me: "I am now asking permission to leave."

The book was definite about that: "Another courtesy of Fijians often extend to each other is a short explanation of where they are going. This is often couched in the form of asking permission. For example, one might say at the end of a short chat with someone on the footpath, "*Sa vinaka, au gole mada ki vei B.P.?*" (If it is all right I am now going to B.P.'s?)"

Father Dobey must have asked if it is all right for us to go to Ba to visit an Indian priest at the Church of Saint Peter Chanel, for that is where we went. The three of us sat in the rectory with a large Bombay fan revolving up near the ceiling and talked about Fijian customs. The priests said that death and birth, and every step between, bring an abundance of ceremonials to every village.

Even at the cutting of the umbilical cord, *vicocico ni gore*, the child's father provides a gift, *magiti*, for the midwife. The cord is buried and a tree planted on the spot, otherwise the child will grow up a restless spirit.

At the other end of life, at death, there are customs galore. For example, after the funeral those who stay behind at the home of the deceased have a ceremony called *Bulu we ni yava*, literally, "burying the footsteps." This is the time to drink the last of the *kava* and to talk about those who have left for home; it is what they say about you then that really counts. Finally, no one is left except the *Bika Bika*, those women who sit from four to ten days after the burial on the spot where the body of the deceased had rested.

In some parts of Fiji on the day of the funeral no movable property is left lying around, not even a hen, because of a custom called *Kerekere*. This custom allows anyone to feel free to take whatever is needed or strikes the fancy.

My hosts told of the missionary who went to a village one evening to preside at the funeral, but by the following afternoon the funeral had not yet taken place. "The grave is not yet dug, your reverence." The missionary, looking into the matter, found four men trying to scrape a hole in the ground with sticks. The chief whispered in his ear: "They're from the next village, Father. They'd take away the spades and have a right to, if we let them use them. It's the custom, Father. *Kerekere*."

This reminded Father Dobey of a custom called *tauvu*, meaning literally, "having the same root or founder." By Fijian custom such people have reciprocal rights when it comes to appropriating one another's goods and swearing at one another.

When sailing to a distant coral island in the Yasawas, for example, one of the boys in Father Dobey's crew pointed to a passing island and said, "Very ignorant people in that village, Father."

"How's that?"

Another member of the crew took up the theme: "Oh, Father, they're very foolish! One of the children asked his mother for the moon and cried so much that some of the villagers went to the top of the hill with a long pole thinking they could knock it down for him."

A third member of the crew said, "Another time they went to that big rock and tried to hollow it out for a boat."

The skipper explained to the missionary that this is an example of *tauvu*, having a common ancestor god. Since these boys were somewhat related to the people of the village, they could poke fun at them and get by with it—like teasing someone you like.

With the curiosity of the outsider I asked the priests about the dark side of Fijian history: What about the custom that gave this archipelago the title of the Cannibal Isles?

This reminded my hosts of the ten-day trek across the mountains that Archbishop Petero Mataca had made recently to offer a Mass of Reconciliation at Nabutautau. The people there felt cursed by an act of cannibalism committed 110 years earlier.

On Sunday morning, July 21, 1867, a Methodist missionary, accompanied by some students, had set out from Nabutautau to visit hill tribes, many of whom still practiced cannibalism. Members of the party marched in single file through tall jungle grass escorted by a chief and his men. Suddenly the escort turned on the missionary and clubbed him and several students to death. Two students, escaping into the tall reeds, lived to tell the tale. The bodies of the victims, an historian related, "were taken to Chubue where they were cut up and cooked."

Father Dobery and the Indian priest, finding me a willing listener, told how when a chief or warrior died, his wife or wives used to be strangled to accompany his spirit to a land called Bulu. If many warriors were slain in battle an equal number of women back in the village had loops put around their necks by relatives.

Now that my hosts were warming to the dark side of Fijian lore, they described how whenever a gigantic boat was built and needed to be rolled from the site to the sea, human beings were slaughtered and stretched out in front to make it slide more readily.

Because of the influence of missionaries, a boat was launched in 1853 without using human bodies as "rollers." The natives felt the boat was jinxed because on its maiden voyage to the village of the great chief, Cakobou, the mast fell and killed a man. The chief agreed that this misfortune happened because the boat builders had neglected to have human rollers at the launching. To rectify the oversight he had twenty-one men slaughtered for sacrifice.

During my introduction to Fijian lore Father Dobey and I used the Columban parish in Lautoka as our base of operation. There the mission compound includes a church, rectory, convent, parish hall and five school buildings for 600 pupils.

Of the 2,500 Catholics in the parish, most are Fijians. The 600 Indian parishioners comprise the largest concentration of Indian Catholics in Fiji.

After about a week we started traveling a rough road, the 315-mile circuit of the island of Viti Levu. The northern section, the 164 miles from Suva back to Lautoka, is especially discouraging.

"One good thing about that part of the road, it is bad all the way," a Columban said. He paused to let me ponder that before explaining, "So you are not always looking forward to the good bits."

Perhaps even worse than the sorry surface of the road are the everchanging hazards that dot the route: the Fijian lying prone in the middle of a narrow bridge, the yoke of oxen that refuse to give the right of way with any sort of alacrity, the Indian driver changing a tire while parked in the road on a curve. As a Columban said of this road, "You respect it."

Along the route we visited grade schools, high schools and a college where Columbans work. We stopped at parish rectories where missionaries helped me learn more and more about a dark, deep, complex culture.

Eventually we made the forty-five minute flight from Suva to Labasa, on Vanua Levu. After being delayed in Suva airport by faulty equipment, things went well enough until we hit an updraft or a downdraft over the mountains. Suddenly, we were riding a bucking bronco. The plane lurched and fishtailed. Somehow or other the wings did survive such wrenching, twisting, tossing.

Life on Vanua Levu is less sophisticated than that on Viti Levu. We bounced across a confusion of dirt roads, stopping from time to time at remote houses to ask directions. We worked our way up into the jungle bush, past mangrove swamps and rain forests. Suddenly, we would come across a mission compound carved from a dense forest. What lonely spots!

How do missionaries handle loneliness? The question haunted me until I asked Father Dobey about it.

"When I came here I was full of life, and young, and very busy," he replied. "I had a big family in Ireland that I enjoyed, but I did not get homesick. Now that I am in Australia I miss Fiji more than I miss Ireland."

I asked a Marist who lives on a remote island if he had experienced loneliness during his thirty-four years in Fiji. "You will always feel alone on the shore," he said. "Alone but not lonely."

·22·

No More the Leper's Bell

Someone told me that when you shake hands with lepers they are alert as to whether or not you flinch. That bit of information stuck in my head, but I never expected to have any use for it. Yet when the time did come that I needed it, it was easy enough to control muscles in hand and arm so as not to flinch outwardly, but something deep inside did recoil. Surely the lepers were sensitive enough to be aware of that.

I was not at ease when I went with Father Dobey to Twomey Memorial Hospital for lepers at Suva, in Fiji. I wanted to meet Semisi Maya, a patient with a far-flung reputation as a watercolorist. When approaching him I told myself not to finch, but found he had scarcely any hands to shake; it was more a matter of grasping the wrist.

Some years ago when there was talk of corrective surgery Semisi asked, "What if you do and I cannot paint?" The surgeon would make no predictions and so the idea was abandoned. The artist sees his affliction as a gift from God: "If it had not been for my sickness none of these things would have happened."

Semisi found his destiny when a nun at the hospital started an art workshop. "Things were pretty depressing in those days," she said. "We wanted to start an occupational-therapy department but there was no money in the budget for that. So we encouraged the patients to work with whatever was available—laundry starch for paint, chips of wood for carving."

Semisi showed a special talent. Working with watercolors is easier than oils because it is so difficult to hold a brush. An associate smears basic colors on paper and the artist blends them using his elbow, the sides of his forearms and wrists. Some of the broader designs are made with joints of the knuckles; for fine lines he grasps a small instrument with both wrists, one interlocked with the other.

When the patients had an exhibit in the Suva town hall, Semisi's water-colors attracted such attention that they were shown in the New York World's Fair in 1965. Soon the Bond Street Galleries in London became agents for all his work. When Raymond Burr, the actor, bought an island in Fiji and built a church for the islanders, he had it decorated with wood-work carved by lepers inspired by Semisi.

Semisi Maya—his name means James the Happy—was struck by leprosy at age twenty-one and sent to the island leprosarium of Makogai, a name that brought fear to the heart as did Molokai a century earlier. Leprosy took the lives of three missionaries on Makogai before an effective cure through the use of Sulphetrone was found in 1948. Within twenty years the population of the island was reduced from 700 to 174. Most of those remaining, Semisi among them, were transferred to the new hospital in Suva.

A missionary who worked among the lepers of Makogai, Father Lucien Soubeyran, is still a legend in the South Pacific. After leaving his native France as a newly ordained priest in 1905 he never returned home. Hardly had he reached the South Seas when he contracted filariasis, a disease carried by mosquitos, causing fever and swelling which leads to elephantiasis, an enlargement of the limbs. Even with the handicap the French priest still tramped across his mission daily, and later rode a bicycle.

Father Soubeyran, nearing ninety, felt too old to go with the lepers when they left the island for their new home in Suva. He continued rising at 4:40 A.M. and, descending the steep hill to the church, to meditate until Mass at 6:00 A.M. and then give the Eucharist to a few remaining lepers.

He had lived through the old days when in the early stages the leper's features swelled and assumed a peculiar frowning aspect suggesting the face of a lion. In the next stage face and body were disfigured by loathsome ulcers that gave off a sickening odor. Ulcers invaded eyes and throat destroying eyeballs and vocal chords. The extremities became useless and decayed.

I heard about the trauma that a priest and a brother had suffered when visiting the leprosarium. They wanted to turn and run when surrounded by hundreds of the malformed in various stages of putrefaction.

"Its poor victims do not die and rot; they rot and die," said the priest. "We tried to speak to them in cheerful tones, but sheer pity broke the words on our lips. We felt like bursting into tears.

"You can imagine how I felt when the parish priest rode by on a bicycle on his way to anoint some poor soul fortunate enough to be dying. He insisted on anointing every person; he refused to allow his young curate to take the risk.

"And the Sisters, how they astonished us! They worked amid the sight and stench of putrefying bodies and seemed in excellent spirits. They were in snow-white habits dressing with gentle hands the festering sores. It was their sole employment all day every day."

Nuns did more than anyone to help the lepers. A bishop wrote to the chief medical officer in Fiji: "Sister Emilie is not yet very well, as she is still losing part of her meals. I expect it is the air they breathe over the tub where they clean the leper's wounds that tells on the health of many of the Makogai nuns."

In a book about such work on the island, Sister Stella wrote: "The odor was almost unbearable, and even their fellow patients would refuse to approach them. Caring for them was the special task of the Sisters."

A two-sentence exchange of conversation on the island has become quoted over the world: A visitor told a Sister, "I wouldn't do that for a million dollars." The Sister replied, "Neither would I."

After I had met Semisi and had looked at his watercolors, the director of the leper hospital, Sister Virginia Matthews of Lowell, Massachusetts, showed me around. She and other Missionary Sisters of Mary care for fifty-two patients in the hospital and for hundreds of outpatients. About twenty-five new cases arrive each year. If caught early enough the disease can be cured, but many lepers in remote villages wait too long to seek help.

Father Dobey reminded Sister Virginia that upon visiting Makogai he had met a beautiful young American nun who would refuse to shake hands for fear of passing along her leprosy. She is now back in the United States, said Sister Virginia.

I heard the story of Louisa, a young Indian woman in Fiji, who dreaded to leave the colony. At eight she had contracted leprosy and had been sent to Makogai where the Sisters taught her to sew, a skill she mastered despite shortened and twisted fingers. And she became something of a linguist: In the polyglot colony she picked up Fijian, Tongan and a few other South Seas languages; in turn, she taught Hindustani to the patients.

A new drug cured her, in 1951, and she was dismissed. With the marks of the disease upon her she returned to a world that had little interest in ex-lepers. Then came a ray of hope: She found a sore on her foot—maybe it was leprosy! When the doctor told her it was just an ordinary sore, Louisa broke into tears. She wanted an excuse to return to the island.

The doctor told the Mother Superior at Makogai and the nun invited

Louisa to come live in the convent. "This is your home as long as you care to stay," were the happiest words the young woman had ever heard.

Yet she had grown so accustomed to not being wanted that she could not bring herself to believe fully in her good fortune. The nun said that she was almost afraid to approach Louisa to speak to her. "Her face fills with terror. She thinks, this is it! That she is being sent away."

Lepers had seemed as remote as the Old Testament until I went to Korea to write the biography of Archbishop Harold Henry. He had done so much for them that a colony is named in his honor.

When he arrived in Korea as a newly ordained priest from Minnesota, in 1933, Harold Henry was appalled to hear that there were 30,000 lepers in that country. He saw them as the most needy and established a colony, providing housing and livestock for 400 families. His were the most needy lepers of them all, the burnt-out cases who had been forced out of the leprosarium. A burnt-out case is a leper who is cured after the disease has eaten away everything that can be eaten away. Such cases are not accepted in society; they are too disfigured.

The archbishop provided financial aid for three other leper colonies. While money was hard to come by, even harder to find were helping hands. To work for lepers takes a special grace. One of Harold Henry's confreres said: "The lepers are sensitive and quick to notice that a priest does not shrink from them. When they are being baptized or confirmed, all watch the minister of the sacrament closely to see if he will touch them, and their hearts are won when he does. A missionary has no place in a leprosarium unless he is able to overcome his repugnance to the point where he can advance without shuddering. Knowing this, Archbishop Henry never assigned a missionary to a leper colony without more than usual deliberation."

The archbishop was haunted by the need for helping hands. A few Caritas Sisters volunteered, but more were needed. On a visit to Pusan he met a visiting bishop from Austria and spoke with such feeling about lepers that the visitor went 400 miles out of his way to see a leper colony. Appalled, he returned to Austria and spoke of the experience with such feeling that three Austrian nurses went out to Korea to establish a nursery for nonleper children of leprous parents.

The nurses began their work at the largest leper colony in the world, located on Sorokdo, a beautifully wooded island in the Yellow Sea, a half-mile off the coast of southern Korea. Many of the 5,500 lepers there live in their own small homes, grouped in seven villages, where they garden and raise pigs and chickens. Only the most serious cases are kept in the hospital.

One of the nurses described the first time she attended Mass in the church on Sorokdo: "A man, swinging both arms for balance, briskly slid forward on some padding tied to his knees. Another middle-aged blind man felt his way along the wall to the front, apparently counting each window until he knew where to crouch in his place. From behind came a sound that was odd for an August morning—the distinct rhythmic crunch of footsteps on snow. It was produced by the wad of bandages added to the stub of an old lady's foot."

Although a cure was found for the disease—weekly use of D.D.S. tablets—leprosy still remains a psychological problem. A pamphlet about it says: "Within the limits of normality, every individual loves himself. In cases where he has a deformity or abnormality or develops it later, his own aesthetic sense revolts and he develops a sort of disgust toward himself. Though with time he becomes reconciled to his deformities, it is only at the conscious level. His subconscious mind, which continues to bear the mark of the injury, brings about certain changes in his whole personality, making him suspicious of society."

Despair is the affliction a chaplain in a leprosarium helps his people fight against. Some try to escape through drugs and some through suicide.

Grim as it is, leprosy is one human agony that has been tempered by new drugs and a more kindly attitude. Years ago in Fiji, for example, lepers were smoked over a fire of a poisonous shrub, *sinu gaga*, which grows near the beach. The milky juice from the leaves is so deadly that a little in the eye causes blindness. Some lepers suffocated in the process. Those who nearly died, but did not do so readily, were clubbed to death.

The leper's bell is gone for good. And so is the cry, "Unclean! Unclean!" The new status of lepers is just one of the many changes Martin Dobey has seen since arriving in Fiji in 1952. We spoke of various changes as he drove me to the airport for my departure.

I asked Father Dobey what are the biggest changes. He answered without hesitation: "The decline of old values."

"That has happened all over the world," I said.

"It's different here," he said. "In most places the family ties have weakened, but Fijian culture was never built around the family. It was always centered in the tribe. The chief.

"Nowadays," said Father Dobey, "the older people shake their heads at the way the younger ones see things. As a poetic Fijian put it, 'many traditions that used to give cohesion to life have vanished like the evening smoke above the village.'"

We said good-bye at the door of the custom's room. I told Father Dobey that my intuitions had been superb when in Ireland I suggested that we meet in Fiji. Fijians, Indians and Europeans had assured me throughout the trip that even with years of searching I could not have found a better companion for a journey around the islands.

The pioneers in the American West had an expression: "He's a good man to have along."

·23·

The China Story

As I said earlier, while waiting in Navan for the Columbans to read the Burma manuscript I suggested to Father Dobey that we meet in Fiji within a year. The following day a note arrived from Mother Catherine Hurley, superior general of the Columban Sisters, saying that she would like to have me tell the story of the work the Columban Sisters had done in China.

When we met a few days later she said that the Sisters had gone out to China in 1926 and had stayed until expelled by the Reds in 1951. The China she spoke of was the one I had known during the Second World War and had little resemblance to that of today. So visiting there would have little value in the research. I would need to interview elderly nuns about their experiences along the Yangtze and look into the archives at Magheramore, in County Wicklow. I promised to write the book she wanted, but could not start until after completing the manuscript about Fiji.

In 1945 Archbishop Harold Henry and I had visited Magheramore, the old-fashioned country house that serves as world headquarters for the Missionary Sisters of Saint Columban. The archbishop wanted to visit an old priest living in the gatehouse. Father Hugh Sands had given most of his life to China, the archbishop said, and was now chaplain to the Columban Sisters.

We found the pixie-like priest, with white exploding hair, black bushy eyebrows and great expressive eyes, sitting in front of an inadequate flame that flickered in an open fireplace. As a defense against the dampness he wrapped himself in a voluminous black cape.

While drinking cups of strong tea the two missionaries recalled their days of adventure—the archbishop's in Korea and the chaplain's in China.

The conversation was drawing to a close when the archbishop told the chaplain a story about an elderly missionary, a mutual friend of theirs, now retired in the United States: The old missionary had stood before his confreres on a cold winter morning with a shovel in hand, speaking of a young priest he had worked with in China long years ago.

"Ah yes, he suffered a martyr's death," said the retired missionary. "They tied him behind wild horses. Dragged him to death. A martyr he was! Indeed! And here I am shoveling snow."

With sad amusement Archbishop Henry and Father Sands repeated the final line. They felt empathy with it. Adventure had gone out of their lives, too. In comparison with the dramatic days of their youth they were just "shoveling snow."

It was not until five years later, when doing research about the Columban Sisters, that I learned what a remarkable man Father Sands was. A couple of anecdotes stand out in my mind:

One of them starts at five in the morning, early in August 1931, when the dikes broke on the Yangtze River. Cholera followed soon afterward. The disease was so infectious that corpses had to buried immediately. Carpenters worked around the clock making coffins.

Besides taking a stand against cholera, the Columban Sisters were treating refugees for smallpox, dysentery, beriberi, scarlet fever, influenza and typhoid. Father Sands, who had the gift of a great reporter, stopped by their hospital in Hanyang and told them that across the river in Hankow 8,000 people had drowned the night the dikes broke. Only the roofs of many houses show above the water, he said, and human corpses and dead animals float in what seems a vast, tideless sea. The water has brought destitution to 23 million people.

He was hurrying to his mission in Chi Woo Tai, he said, to be there in time for the Feast of the Assumption. The nuns, concerned about floods and bandits, asked him to delay his trip. The wiry little priest did not see it as an unreasonable risk.

For eight days Father Sands traveled by water past millions of refugees. Upon reaching his church at Chi Woo Tai he found parishioners living atop anything that would float. The first thing they told him was that the Reds had landed in more than a hundred boats at a village two miles away.

The exhausted priest went to the top floor of his house to take a nap. No sooner had he fallen asleep than a boy ran into the room crying, "The Reds are here!" A bandit, screaming at the top of his voice, crashed through the door brandishing a revolver.

For the next few days Father Sands found himself in a convoy of fifty boats, each manned by four Reds. At every village the Communists made demands and the villagers obeyed. One person must contribute fifty dollars, another a hundred. It was evident the Reds knew how much each one could afford.

When the convoy reached camp, atop a hill outside a pretty village, the Reds drove a contingent of Chinese army soldiers from the place. Years later Father Sands would say, "That was the day I learned that working for an ideal gives more power than working for money. The Reds were driven by an ideal; the government soldiers cared mainly about collecting their pay."

Since Father Sands was the first Caucasian ever seen in those parts, he had to endure the humiliation of being inspected. The villagers examined his clothes, rubbed his hair and pawed him all over. One examination was not enough: The curious returned each day and brought friends who also found the stranger amusing. Amid giggles they asked a thousand times his name, age, occupation and home country.

Father Sands endured all of this unsought attention in the ruins of an ancient temple atop a hill. The room in which he was held was spacious during the day, but at night he had to share it with donkeys, mules and horses, thirty in all. As the animals milled around, the missionary tried to sleep on a plank, fourteen inches wide by five feet in length, placed atop several bricks.

Anyone opposing the Reds was immediately executed. Hugh Sands witnessed a dozen such deaths. The one he found most painful to watch was the crucifixion of a man to a tree with the bandit rubbing salt water into the victim's wounds saying, "This is how to treat a spy."

The Reds hurried to their boats one evening when they feared a large military force was about to attack. In the confusion Father Sands slipped away and hid in a house. An old man living there led him through several flooded rooms, out through a flooded yard, up a ladder and over a wall. The two of them climbed onto a floating door and paddled to a neighboring house. In a flooded room the old man placed a stool atop a table and had the missionary sit on it.

Within minutes the Reds had found their prisoner. Strangely enough, at no time did they make any reference to his attempt to escape.

Back in Hanyang the nuns gathered bits and pieces of information about the priest's condition in captivity. Since rural China was a gigantic grapevine, word was passed along about the foreign captive, but how much of it could be believed was something else.

The nuns were wary of what they heard because they had learned that to get a message delivered in China took some doing. The only sure way to reach the recipient was to deliver it yourself.

No matter how carefully the messenger was selected and no matter with what good intentions he set out, "the way was long." When tired he would ask a friend who was "going near the place" to take the message. The friend also became tired—as the Chinese say, "*Sceeang fa tze*" (he looked for a way out)—and he, too, passed the message to a friend who was "going just beside the place." Eventually the message was distorted, or reached the wrong person or was never delivered to anyone.

The Sisters did put trust in the information brought back by Mah Shien Sin. He was a teacher who often risked his life interviewing the Reds to secure the release of missionaries. When Mah returned to Hanyang he said that the Reds had asked Father Sands to write for guns, but that the priest had convinced them it was a futile request. They demanded that he write for 3,000 pounds, but he refused to do that, too. Finally, both sides agreed on 300 pounds and the missionary wrote to Bishop Edward Galvin. Since no answer came, the Reds had him write another letter. When Mah arrived at the Red camp he learned that neither letter had been sent and no one could explain why.

The Reds took Father Sands on a three-day journey to a village near Red Lake. The Soviet headquarters had been moved there when the islands in Red Lake became flooded.

In the village everyone seemed antiforeign, except for a Chinese Red with the improbable name of White. Whenever White took the priest for a walk, a taunting mob followed. The mob became so threatening on one occasion that had it not been for two Reds with revolvers the priest might well have been murdered. Thereafter White and the missionary did not take their walks until after dark.

Father Sands lived on the edge of starvation through the fall of 1931. When he seemed sufficiently weakened by hunger and loneliness, the Reds said that if he would apostatize they would free him immediately.

"Would you renounce your communism and join the government army?" he asked.

"Certainly not," they said.

"Then you know how I feel."

This seemed to appeal to his captors. Perhaps that is why they brought in Father Lazzeri, an Italian Franciscan, and allowed the two priests to talk for a few minutes each day. Father Sands decided, however, that the Reds were doing him no favors because the Franciscan was so pessimistic that all he did was to make the day seem darker than it already was.

Father Lazzeri said that he had written a letter for his ransom, a supply of medicines. When the Reds asked Father Sands to write for medicines, he did so.

One day a guard came to Father Sands and said, "You are free to go. Your ransom is here."

"What about him?" the Columban asked pointing to Father Lazzeri.

"No ransom. He stays."

Father Sands took a look at the old Franciscan. Without medical attention and better food he would not last another month.

"Let him go instead." Even as he said it he wondered why he was doing it. As he said later, "I didn't even like the fellow."

Father Sands began slipping out notes, some of which eventually reached Hanyang. He described being crowded into a room with sixty-six other prisoners, men and women, all of whom were held for ransom. The place was filthy and infected with vermin and rats. "There are," he wrote, "two buckets in two corners of the room, with no screens, and they are the W.C."

Finally, on May 9, 1932, five months after his capture, Father Sands was released.

Back in Hanyang it was evident he needed medicine and substantial food. The Sisters provided both. As they nursed him back to health they were aware of one of the notes that he had sent from Red Lake: "Nothing dries more quickly than a tear."

When Mao Tse-tung died, in September of 1976, I was in Killiney. Suddenly, Father Hugh Sands was being quoted in newspapers all over Ireland and was a popular guest on radio and television talk shows. Newspapermen and broadcasters were visiting him at the gatehouse at Magheramore. They wanted to hear about the Christmas afternoon Mao had visited him in his cell.

Father Sands told them that in December of 1931 he was in a village near Red Lake when a ten-year-old boy came to his cell carrying a white rabbit. The boy offered the rabbit as a gift.

"I was half-starved," Father Sands told reporters, "so how was I going to feed the rabbit when I hadn't enough for myself. I thanked him for his good intention and he bowed and went out."

The boy returned next day with a rabbit under each arm and offered the two of them. Again Father Sands refused.

The next day, Christmas Eve, the boy brought a big orange. He peeled it carefully and divided it in two.

"I never tasted anything so wonderful," the old missionary recalled. After the boy had left, someone told the priest that Mao Tse-tung was the child's father.

Mao himself came to visit Father Sands on Christmas afternoon.

"What are you doing in China?" he asked.

Father Sands explained that he was a Catholic missionary trying to spread the Christian faith.

"Wasting your time. We're not interested," said Mao. "Confucius used to say, 'We scarcely know the things of this world; how are we to know the things of another one?'"

After a long pause, Mao asked, "Where are you from?"

"Ireland."

"Oh, England."

"Certainly not. Ireland is an independent country. It has its own language, its own stamps and its own currency."

"Nonsense," said Mao. "Empires do not allow independent countries on their doorsteps. Especially not small countries."

Father Sands decided that here was an occasion when politics and religion were topics to avoid. He began describing the frightful mistakes he had made while learning the Chinese language. He told how he had asked his houseboy to go down and sweep the church and dust the altar. The phonetics he used were correct, but the accent was all wrong. So what he actually said was: "Go burn down the church and curse the altar."

Mao laughed, admitting that he had found English equally difficult.

"We can't, for instance, distinguish between the consonants L, M, N, and R. I can't see any difference between 'lend me your knife,' and 'lend me your wife.'"

The conversation continued in such a light vein throughout Christmas afternoon. At dusk Mao bowed out.

After Mao's death, Father Sands, always a "China watcher," approved of the changes that began taking place in the People's Republic. We talked about these when I spent three weeks at Magheramore doing research.

Each evening the chaplain came up to the main house to say Mass for the Sisters. By then, well into his eighties, he was very fragile.

One evening I asked if he remembered writing, "Nothing dries more quickly than a tear."

"Did I now!" he exclaimed.

"Yes, you did. And do you still feel that way about life?"

"Yes, yes," he said. "Oh, my, yes, yes!"

Those were the last words I heard him speak. He was saying them as he turned to go down the long driveway toward the gatehouse. Within a year he died.

·24·

A Lady I Wish I Had Met

Standing at her grave in County Wicklow, I wished I had arrived while she was still living. From the tiny cemetery I walked a hundred yards to the large Irish country house, called Magheramore, to talk with several women who had known her well. Later I read letters she had written and looked at photographs taken of her.

The first photograph showed a lovely young girl, the aristocratic Frances Lewis, sitting sidesaddle atop an elegant mare; that was about the time she was presented at Buckingham Palace. In another photograph she was Lady Maloney living with her husband on the Windward Isles where he was governor.

When Sir Alfred died in Italy, in 1913, Pope St. Pius X predicted that Lady Maloney would find a vocation in charitable work, a prediction that came true shortly after the First World War when she helped found the Missionary Sisters of Saint Columban.

That Lady Maloney was a no-nonsense woman shows in letters written while planning the new community in Ireland. In evaluating a candidate she wrote: "She is a girl of deepest piety and great love of the poor and has the necessary sense of the ridiculous which carries one over the small difficulties and worries of daily life." In describing a woman she hoped would be mistress of novices she said: "She has a big mind and a big heart and I think would not worry us with all the pettiness which we would wish to avoid."

Even while organizing the community she studied nursing in Dublin to get ready for her work in China. Then from February 1922 until September 1926 she lived in a remote convent on the River Shannon, in County Clare, experiencing the intensive training required of a future nun.

As Sister Mary Patrick she arrived in Hanyang, China, in November

1926, with five other Sisters. High adventure awaited them. The country was plagued by bandits, civil-war soldiers and Red revolutionaries. The ancient agonies of floods and pestilence recurred like themes in a dramatic tragedy. Poverty and ignorance intensified such daily distress as hunger, leprosy and tuberculosis. Soon the Japanese would invade China and the Second World War would follow thereafter.

During the next ten years Sister Mary Patrick opened clinics, hospitals and schools. Time and again she and the other nuns had to flee bandits and Red revolutionaries. Her letters were filled with the problems all of them faced.

During a flood, for example, a virulent disease, something like cholera, carried off patients within a day's illness. "It killed two of our best Hanyang pupils," she wrote. "One poor woman lost her mind with it."

Whatever the mysterious disease was it flamed like fire, sweeping from camp to camp. The missionaries fought back with a series of injections, inoculating on the average of 900 people a day. The miracle is that all the nuns survived on two sandwiches a day, working long hours in contact with death in the stench of little huts.

In another letter Mother Mary Patrick told of a Chinese woman who swallowed opium in an attempt to kill herself. To reach her, she and Sister Mary Agnes follow a messenger through fetid streets oppressive with humidity. Upon entering a small room crowded with excited neighbors the nuns felt there was no more air left to breathe.

Sister Mary Patrick turned to the woman sprawled on a pad and forced down her throat some mustard in lukewarm water, enough to upset the equilibrium of a dozen normal people, but it brought no results. Permanganate also went down with no effect.

"She must be wakened up," Sister Mary Patrick said. "She mustn't go to sleep or she will die."

Sister Mary Agnes began slapping and pinching the patient. Despite the seriousness of the moment, the nuns could not help but laugh at the sound of the smacking the woman was getting. Sister Mary Agnes asked for a wet towel and was handed one that had been filthy even before being soaked in muddy water. With it she smacked the unconscious woman with such vigor that the crowd showed signs of concern.

After one hour the woman regained her senses enough to resist treatment. The nuns told a couple of able-bodied men to march her up and down the room, or rather drag her for she would not lift her feet. This commandeering of onlookers was an inspiration for it caused the crowd to thin out, allowing some air into the room.

Two days later the Sisters called upon the patient to ask how she felt. She said that her health was improved, but that her whole body was sore and she pulled up her sleeves to show the marks where she had been pinched and slapped. The nuns could hardly keep straight faces; it was evident that the woman did not know they were the culprits.

At the start of Holy Week in 1930, Mother Lelia and Sisters Mary Patrick, Dolores, Michael and Columban left Hanyang by steamer for Sien Tao Chen, 150 miles away. On the trip up the Han, in whichever direction they looked, fore or aft, port or starboard, they saw Chinese junks with high deck, two enormous eyes in the bow, and a single square sail fitted with bamboo laths to prevent its "bellying." Such an exotic setting and a new challenge had everyone in high spirits.

The Sisters arrived in the morning just in time for the ceremonies on Wednesday. That ritual and the remainder of Holy Week were heightened by their participation. Easter Sunday in the church in Sien Tao Chen was the biggest day the Catholics remembered. The church was packed; many could not get in at all. An organ was lent by a pagan in the street, so Sister Mary Patrick played. The other sisters formed the choir and Father Lane, after hearing confessions for five-and-a-half hours, sang a Missa Cantata. The Church was at its height in Sien Tao Chen. Catholics and pagans alike rejoiced to see the Sisters among them. Father Walsh said that the next day when he and Bishop Galvin and Fathers Quinlan, Laffan, Linehan and O'Collins were together, "We concluded that the coming of the Sisters to the country was the crowning of our Mission."

On Thursday night, April 24, Communist bandits secretly surrounded Sien Tao Chen and waited for dawn. At first light they rushed the town from four points, shooting as they came and shouting "*saar!*" (kill). The defenders, still in bed, gave scant resistance and so the brigands took possession and began looting.

When rifle fire began, Bishop Galvin was at the Communion of the Mass. With him were Father Walsh and Sisters Columban and Michael. Soon Fathers O'Collins and Linehan, having scaled the wall at the rear of the compound, went to the altar to consume the Blessed Sacrament. Mother Lelia hurried out, followed by Sister Dolores, who instantly returned to the convent for Sister Mary Patrick. When all priests and nuns gathered in the church, they went into the sacristy, for it afforded the best protection against bullets.

A commotion outside drew Bishop Galvin to the church door. Two dozen Reds shouted for admittance at the front gate. Suddenly, they broke into the compound.

The bishop moved to the center of the church to stand his ground. The young bandit leader, Wang, came forward with a smile. He was neatly dressed in a military uniform and spoke with the politeness of a gentleman.

Wang assured the bishop that there was nothing to fear. "We are only against the rich people who oppress the poor. We have no quarrel with the Catholic Church. You priests are good people who help the poor."

The chief had a look around the church and posted guards so that no Columban might escape. Little by little the firing ceased outside the building, or rather shifted to another part of town.

All of the Columbans left the sacristy and went to the women's catechumenate behind the church. There they found the Chinese women huddled together in a dusky room. The bishop said later, "I distinctly recall the terror which was pictured on their faces."

Sister Mary Patrick suggested that since there was a lull at the moment, why not have some coffee and she went to the kitchen for it. Father Linehan took the sacred vessels from the church and buried them in a heap of sand.

Bishop Galvin wrote: "I had a cup of coffee in my hand—into which Mother Lelia had put a fistful of sugar and was stirring it with a knife—when Father Walsh came in to ask that I go to interview the bandit leader. I met him in front of the church. Again, he was friendly and polite, and I, too—however I may have felt—tried to be likewise. For we were completely in the man's power; any show of harshness might have irritated him and his followers and perhaps cost us our lives."

The bishop said, "You must be very tired. Come, have some breakfast."

Soon the bandit chief was having tea and toast and eggs and chatting with the bishop, as though it were a reunion of old friends.

The bishop asked where the Reds had come from, and the young chief said that he could not tell, but that it was a distance of ninety *li* (thirty miles). This marching all night is wearing, he said.

"The Sisters are frightened," the bishop told him. "All of that shooting."

"They should not be. I will go to them. I will speak to them."

Wang returned to the church where the Sisters had gathered once again and spoke to them kindly. He said that they are good people and have nothing to fear.

In the most polite Chinese fashion he bowed himself out.

Such friendliness brought a vague sense of security. The priests and nuns were in a heightened mood when they went to the Sisters' dining room for breakfast. "It was a pleasant meal, as I recall it now," wrote Bishop Galvin.

"Anyone seeing us there at breakfast together would never have guessed that we were surrounded by bandits. God in his mercy hides the future from us all; it was well we did not know the terrible day that lay ahead of us."

Suddenly the dining-room door flew open and two men with drawn revolvers stood there. One of them, Yuen, took the bishop to an adjoining room while the other kept an eye on the nuns and priests at the table.

Yuen said he had nothing against the Church and that the Columbans had nothing to fear. However, he wanted the priests to come to town with him "to talk things over."

Later the bishop wrote: "I had a suspicion of what that might mean. I did not wish any priest to leave the compound, so I told him it was very inconvenient for me to go, that we had treated them well, that if they had anything to talk over why could they not come to the Mission instead of asking us to go to their headquarters, that we had to protect the church, and that if we went with them everything that we had would be looted."

Just as he made the last point, Father Laffan came to the room to say, "They are breaking up the church."

"You see, what I have told you is true. If we go, they will smash everything in the church."

"No," said Yuen, "I will stop them," and out he went with the bishop and Father Laffan following.

The church was filled with bandits, all looting. They had smashed the statue of Our Lady, a gift of Father Laffan's mother, and it lay about the foot of the altar in a thousand fragments. The statue of the Sacred Heart was broken, too, and the altars stripped of their cloths. The sacristy was a wreck.

Yuen ordered the looters from the church, and he and the bishop and Father Laffan returned to the Sisters' house. At the door the three were joined by two bandits brandishing revolvers. The old argument was resumed, the one about the priests needing to go to town "to talk things over."

Suddenly Yuen turned to Father Laffan: "What's your name? You will have to go!"

The bishop protested, but the priest said, "It's useless. The fellow behind me with the revolver says I must go, and I'll go."

Father Laffan went into the dining room and asked Father O'Collins to give him absolution. He turned to the Sisters and asked that they pray for him.

Upon returning to the front door, where the bishop and the bandits waited, Father Laffan removed his Chinese slippers and, while lacing his shoes, looked up at the bishop, smiled and said, "I'll meet you on the other side of the grave. Write home and tell them about it." As he started to go he whispered, "Whatever I write you, you will know what I *mean*."

The bishop wrote to Father O'Dwyer: "When he had gone about half a dozen paces from the door, he turned again and waved good-bye to me. His face was pale, but he was still smiling.

"To my dying day that awful picture will always be in my mind—the picture of that brave man going out to die and asking me to send a last message to his mother. For, I did not think of you or anyone in the Society, I saw only his mother and she seemed to be before me there with a vividness and a reality which I can neither describe nor analyze.

"So far I had tried to be steady and keep my balance, but now a strange weakness had come over me; I could feel the tears running down my face and there was a choking sensation in my throat. The bandits were all around me, but I didn't see them. I walked up and down the front of the house trying to hold myself in check. After some time I went into the dining room to tell Father O'Collins and the Sisters. I thought I was calm again, but when I began to speak about it, I couldn't go on."

The nuns were steady, but anxiety showed in their faces. "Offer him up to God," said Mother Lelia. "God will take care of him."

Bandits were coming and going in the dining room, grabbing whatever struck their fancy. The bishop told Father O'Collins to take the Sisters into the adjoining room, while he and Fathers Walsh and Linehan remained outside to do whatever they could.

"Our great fear was, what was to become of the Sisters if we were taken off—one by one—as seemed to be the intention of the bandits. Were we to bring the Sisters with us into captivity, or were we to leave them there in the compound surrounded by the bandits? It was a fearful alternative."

The bishop walked around the compound several times looking for a way of escape. There was none. The front gate was well guarded and at the back gate three brigands were dividing the loot. On either side of the compound were groups of riflemen.

As the bishop rejoined Father Linehan, two bandits approached with drawn revolvers, and one said, "Another man must go."

"One of our men has already gone," said the bishop.

"One is not enough. There is a man here named Linn [Father Linehan's Chinese name]. We want him too."

"I'll go," said Father Linehan. He was cool, though his face was pale. He showed no trace of nervousness as he went out, followed by the two bandits, very much as if he was going to some ordinary duty of the day.

It was now 8:30 A.M. The bishop returned to the dining room to tell Father Walsh of the latest defeat.

"What are you doing?" he asked the priest.

"There is no hope. I am writing a letter to Doctor O'Dwyer so that he will know about it."

"If they come for another man, I'll go," said the bishop.

"No, you stay with the Sisters as long as you can. I'll go next, if they come for another man. You stay and save the Sisters, if you can."

Father Laffan's houseboy hurried into the room to warn the bishop to change his soutane. He had heard the bandit say, "The man wearing the clothes with the red trimmings is the superior. We must have him."

Another band of looters came surging into the dining room.

By now Bishop Galvin had lost all his patience. He no longer tried to speak with kindness: "I asked them what harm the Catholic church had done them or anyone in China. I said we had come to teach the people to do good, to tell them about God who had created us all and to help the poor. I put it to them to go to anyone in town and find out if we weren't good men who had always tried to help everyone."

The bandit spokesman said, "Yes, you are good men. And we mean you no harm. But you are in league with the imperialists of Ireland."

"The imperialists of Ireland!" The bishop exploded, "Ireland has never been an imperialistic nation. Ireland has never occupied any country."

"Your soldiers and battleships are here."

"Where?"

"In Hankow and Shanghai."

"You won't find an Irish soldier in all of China."

The looters seemed slightly impressed. The bishop followed up his advantage by asking for the release of the two priests.

The bandit said he could not do that, but would guarantee their safety.

After the looters had taken everything movable from the dining room, one of them, with a revolver, demanded that the bishop open the door to where the nuns were waiting. The bishop went into the room to tell the Sisters that they should go upstairs.

In the stack of medical supplies was a bottle of brandy. Mother Lelia pointed to it and asked, "Shall I bring this?"

"Do!"

As the Sisters began to come from the room, one by one, the bandit stood there pointing a revolver. "They must be searched," he said.

"Mother Lelia held up her shawl for him to see," wrote the bishop, "while all the time she had the bottle of brandy safely tucked under her arm. She never turned a hair. It was too funny for words—the Lord save us!—we had no time for fun."

As soon as the Sisters had gone upstairs, a hoard of bandits rushed into the room grabbing left and right at anything and everything. There was a good deal of medicine in the room which they packed up and took away. The parish registers were there, too; they would have given the Reds the names of every Catholic in the locality. By sheer coolness and diplomacy Father O'Collins succeeded in saving the registers.

The room was so crowded with bandits that the bishop wondered if perhaps some had deserted their posts. So he hurried to the back of the compound and found the rear gate unguarded. It was now or never.

The sentry at the door was still a problem. The bishop told him that with all of the looting the women would be frightened and so he would take them to a different building.

The sentry, meaning to be helpful, shouted to the looters on the upstairs veranda to come down at once. They paid no heed, for which Bishop Galvin was thankful.

In the upstairs room the bishop said to the nuns, "Follow me." That they did in good order and without undue haste.

"We passed the sentry without difficulty, for he had the impression that I was taking them to some other room at the back. He thought that the back gate was still guarded. From the Sisters' compound we passed through the door which led to the women's catechumenate. Fathers O'Collins and Walsh brought up the rear."

The bishop told the houseboy, Ma, to go ahead as a scout. The Columbans followed, slipping from one clump of bushes to another, taking advantage of every strand of trees and every fold in the ground. Ma kept twenty yards ahead, feeling his way, constantly looking for bandits.

Ma sought out faint paths and avoided all roads. The pagans along the way gave all the help they could, suggesting the safest paths.

Some distance out of town the group stopped to rest. The Sisters removed their white headdress for fear it would be too easily seen from a distance.

Just as they started again a bandit came down the road on horseback. On his way to town he passed within fifteen yards of the group but gave no indication of having seen them.

Across the fields they went at a brisk pace, alternating between a fast walk and a trot. With the Han dike in sight hopes mounted. Suddenly Father O'Collins commanded, "Down! They have seen us." Down flat into the wheat went the houseboy, five nuns, two priests and a bishop. Peering through the blades they saw six bandits, with rifles slung on shoulders, about a hundred yards away.

When the bandits had passed, the group crossed the dike of the Han and took a rest within a dense clump of trees. Everyone was surprised when Sister Michael produced from the folds of her robes Mother Lelia's bottle of brandy. She even produced the scissors with which to open the bottle. Bishop Galvin wrote, "Every priest and Sister had a sip as it passed around and it gave us new life and courage."

A boatman said, "Are you fleeing? Get in!" and took them across the Han. The group walked three miles down river and finally found two boats that would take them toward Hanyang.

"It should be borne in mind that we had eaten nothing since early morning and it was now five in the evening, so we bought some Chinese bread and some boiled eggs and had a pleasant if simple meal on board, as our boats went down river.

"No words of mine can convey the glorious spirit of comradeship which bound together that little fugitive band and the fortitude and courage which the Sisters displayed throughout that terrible day. They were simply wonderful. The awful agony which they went through can never be put into words. Nor can any of us ever cease thanking God, for it was He who led them out to safety."

The bishop disembarked in the darkness several miles below Sien Tao Chen. Everyone urged him to continue on to Hanyang, but he insisted on returning to the mission compound, saying that from there he would be better able to work for the release of Fathers Laffan and Linehan. Seven months passed before he could get them released.

And so it went day after day, one adventure after another, and before Sister Mary Patrick knew it ten years had passed. When she left for Ireland, not expecting to stay there long, she carried with her the satisfaction of knowing the Sisters were doing remarkable work.

Hardly had she reached the convent in County Clare than she was elected superior general, a position she would have preferred to avoid. Three more years passed and war was flaring out all over the world. Although aware of the dangers of wartime travel, she was determined to get from Ireland to China, feeling the need to make an official visit, especially with everything so chaotic.

Of her journey through countries at war she wrote: "I can still visualize the shadowy forms of the worshipers at early Mass in London and Paris churches to which we found our way by flashlight. Paris was not blacked out so completely as London was. In the French capital a delicate shade of peacock blue pervaded the city.

"In the sunny land of Italy we found worshipers on bended knees at the same holy Mass. Here, as elsewhere, mothers and wives were pleading before the throne of God for the safety of their dear ones."

By Christmas Eve, 1939, she had reached the Philippines and attended Mass in a chapel near Manila. She would recall years later that the celebrant was one of the six Columban fathers who would be killed in the Philippines later in the war.

By the time Mother Mary Patrick reached China, early in 1940, Japanese armies had occupied all the cities of the coast—Shanghai, Canton, Tientsin, Peking—and all the cities of the Yangtze Valley up to Hanyang.

In Hanyang she could not help but compare past with present: "Many of the streets are masses of ruins and places one remembers as dotted with houses have been transformed into large open spaces, for all of the building material has been carried away."

She was pleased to note how much Catholicism had spread since her departure four years earlier. The enlargement of the cathedral she saw as symbolic: It had been extended to twice the length that she remembered. She could remember when there had been 120 Catholics in the city and now there were 6,000. The bishop told her that the inhabitants of hundreds of villages had been converted. "An entire countryside is moving toward the Church," he said, and added, "Calamities are forerunners of waves of grace."

Each evening when the nuns gathered in the convent and talked about the events of the day, Mother Mary Patrick was reminded of similar stories she had exchanged during her ten years there. For example, a Sister said: "Today a child fell from a loft onto a basin. He received a nasty gash on the head. The wound bled profusely until we put in a few stitches. The gratitude of the parents was touching."

Mother Mary Patrick was touched daily by the gratitude she received. An old woman, for example, brought a basket of eggs, saying that years ago the nun had saved her husband's life.

In a farewell concert, when the superior general was ready to return to County Clare, the sisters sang: "Killarney," "Vale of Avoca," and "Hills of Donegal," escaping momentarily, as one of them said, "from the grim realities of China to the fair hills of holy Ireland."

The most dramatic experience of the superior general's wartime tour came on the way home. When she and her traveling companion, Sister Eileen Muldoon of Chicago, boarded the British ship, *Western Prince*, in New York harbor, December 4, 1940, they heard that the sailing had been postponed nearly twenty-four hours.

In the darkness before dawn, the next morning, the two nuns came cautiously down the icy gangplank on their way to find a church. As they were asking a night watchman to call a taxi, an Irish policeman came along and added his whistle to form a duet. The cab driver, expressing surprise at seeing nuns on the waterfront at such an hour, took them to the nearest church, Sacred Heart.

After attending the seven and eight o'clock Masses, they crossed the street and had breakfast in the convent. There they met an elderly Irish lady, Mary O'Brien, from County Clare, who wept tears of joy at the sight of someone who knew well the hills of home. As the Sisters prepared to leave for the ship, Mary O'Brien exclaimed, "God stand between you and harm!" an appropriate prayer considering what was ahead.

At the head of the icy gangplank the captain greeted the nuns and commented on the inadvisability of their making a sea voyage in these times. He was aware, in this the second winter of the war, that German U-boats frequently roamed the North Atlantic and that many ships went down.

"Missionaries, like sailors, must take risks," said the superior general. The captain spoke no more of danger.

On ship the nuns became friends with Dr. Dorothy Galbraith, herself a missionary. The three women spoke of China with such affection that other passengers began to tease them, calling them the Old China Hands.

When Dr. Galbraith and the Sisters were assigned to the same lifeboat during the ship's drill, they helped each other adjust life jackets. During a class in first aid the ship's doctor suggested a method for treating hysterics: Knock the hysteric over the head lest the condition become contagious.

Mother Mary Patrick brought out of her luggage several religious medals. The captain accepted one. Another officer declined, assuring her that Saint Christopher was good enough for him. A Catholic stewardess brought up the first officer who asked for a medal and pinned it beneath his lapel.

As a community of two, the nuns were as exacting in their spiritual duties on the high seas—following the Ordinary and the Proper of the Mass each day—as though they were in a convent. After saying their prayers, Friday night, December 13, they retired early.

A torpedo struck at a quarter of six the next morning. It passed through the ship which shivered and stood still.

Sister Eileen, having fallen from her bunk, jumped up and said, "Mother, what was that!"

The nuns hurried into their habits, quickly adjusted life belts, and seized cloaks and shawls. They were literally thrown into the lifeboat. As the first officer commanded, "Let down the boats!" the captain cried out, "Pull off and good luck!"

Rain, sleet and icy spray swept over the passengers in the open boats, which seemed so fragile riding the deep troughs of the high seas. Fifty minutes after the first torpedo, a second struck the *Western Prince*. The ship burst into flames and began slipping slowly into the sea. From the bright flare in the darkness came three long, slow blasts of a foghorn, the captain's way of saying farewell.

"Some of the sailors tried to keep up their spirits by swearing and joking," recalled Mother Mary Patrick. "After a time I ventured to suggest it would be well to say a prayer, for only God could save us. I started the Our Father and many of them joined in.

"After that we sang hymns. At twelve noon we said the Angelus. Soon after this we heard them call out, 'Ship ahead!'"

The freighter, not seeing the lifeboats, began diminishing on the horizon. The sailors rowed in pursuit like demons. After what seemed an eternity, a lookout on the freighter, scanning the sea for submarines, sighted the lifeboats.

It took two hours to reach the ship. Getting everyone aboard was hazardous, for high waves slammed the small boats against the ship. One lifeboat capsized and its passengers perished. The ship's captain ordered oil thrown overboard to make the waves less rough.

"On deck we were greeted by a fellow passenger imploring us to say whether we had seen his wife," wrote Mother Mary Patrick. "Alas! this bright young creature whom we had admired and spoken to on a few occasions had gone down. A roll call revealed that six passengers and eleven crewmen had perished."

Four days later the ship reached port. Buses carried the survivors to Glasgow. "Like two bedraggled seabirds we eventually arrived in Dublin," said Mother Mary Patrick. "We left next day for County Clare and reached our convent at 8:00 P.M., Friday, December 20, 1940. The Sisters were all assembled in the hall to welcome us."

After the war the Columbans opened missions in Hong Kong, Burma, Korea, Peru, Chile and the Philippines. But in China, where the Sisters had survived bandits, warlords and the plague, the Communists took over and expelled them in 1951.

This was a disappointment, of course, but Mother Mary Patrick took an attitude toward it similar to the one an Irish bishop took. He had given many years to China and when he was eighty-one someone asked, "If you had foreseen the catastrophe in China would you have gone anyway? Or would you have stopped in your tracks?"

He considered this a moment and decided he would have gone anyway: "The harvest that was garnered was immense. The good seed remains in the ground for a second spring."

I visited Magheramore in the summer of 1982 carrying the manuscript of the book, *Maybe a Second Spring*. For the last time I visited the grave of Frances Lewis, who became Lady Maloney, who became Mother Mary Patrick. The stone records the day of her death as August 15, 1959. Her husband had died in 1913. What an admirable way she had spent the forty-six years of her widowhood!

·25·

Japan's Neroes and Heroes

The inner push to write about religion in Japan came from a novel. Since my interest in fiction has faded, it was improbable that a friend, who knows my reading habits, should give me a copy of Shusaku Endo's *Silence*. Even more improbable was that I would read it and, what's more, read it twice.

The novel, which tells of the Nero-like persecutions in Japan, started me researching the story of Christianity in the islands from Saint Francis Xavier to the present. The Columbans, I found, fit into the last fifty years of those four centuries.

One piece of research led to another and finally there I was in Tokyo airport searching the crowd, hoping to recognize a man known only through correspondence. He spotted me first because I had written that I would probably be the only man on the flight from San Francisco wearing a hat.

Father Kevin Flinn grabbed my baggage and hurried to the airport bus with a zest that belied his sixty-three years. My apprehensions began to fade. We will get along just fine, I told myself; the vibrations are good. There was a twinkle in the eye of the handsome Australian priest, one that suggested that he is amused with the world as God created it.

Since Christianity reached Japan at Nagasaki, and the persecutions in Endo's novel took place there, that seemed the place to start. So Father Flinn and I flew the thousand miles from Tokyo to Nagasaki. In that tragic city of rubble Father Flinn had begun his work in 1947.

The two of us climbed the long flight of steps on the slope of Oura Hill to reach the episcopal residence of the Archdiocese of Nagasaki. Father Flinn had once lived in the nicely proportioned red brick house, two stories with verandas stretching across the front.

In the formal parlor a young Japanese priest greeted us. "The cardinal is ill," he said. Father Flinn asked the young priest to deliver a present to the cardinal, a bottle of brandy. The young man returned within minutes and hurried us up the stairs down a long stretch of red carpet to meet Joseph Cardinal Asajiro Satowaki. He and Father Flinn greeted each other with a warmth that showed they were friends of long standing. The cardinal's jet hair, firm face, high cheekbones and lively eyes suggested that he was a decade younger than his seventy-nine years.

The three of us settled at a low table where on February 26, 1981, his eminence had entertained Pope John Paul II. A nun brought strong coffee and slices of sponge cake made from a recipe that had arrived from Portugal 300 years ago.

The cardinal said that he had told the pope that when he was a young priest in Rome, before the Second World War, he met a young Polish Franciscan, Father Maximilian Kolbe, who was about to set out for China to start a magazine. The Japanese priest informed the Franciscan about bandits and warlords and other things that made China an impossible place. Go to Japan, said Father Satowaki, go to Japan!

Father Kolbe took the advice, came to Nagasaki and built a few wooden huts high on a hill. Soon he set up a small press and began publishing a magazine.

The cardinal was pleased that Pope John Paul, twenty months after his visit to Nagasaki, presided over the canonization of his fellow Pole. By then Father Kolbe had become known all over the world for things he did after returning to Poland from Japan. He had harbored Jewish refugees and had spoken out against Nazism and so was a marked man when Hitler invaded Poland in 1939.

In prison Kolbe shared meager rations with others and spent time comforting them. Some survivors say that he inspired them to go on living even in Auschwitz.

When a prisoner escaped from Auschwitz, in July 1941, the commandant arbitrarily selected ten men to be starved to death. One of them, a Polish Jew, cried out for his wife and two children. Kolbe, then forty-seven, offered to take the man's place.

With prayers Father Kolbe continued to console his fellow prisoners. After he had survived two weeks without food or water, a prison guard killed him with an injection.

Among the 150,000 worshipers who attended the ceremony of canonization in Saint Peter's Square was Francizek Gajowniczek, the man whose life Kolbe had saved. After the rite was completed, the pope came forward, embraced and kissed the eighty-one-year-old man who had wept silently through the service. He said to the pope: "I was never able to thank him, but we looked into each other's eyes before he was led away."

The pope, while the guest of Cardinal Satowaki, spoke of another Pole in Japan he wanted to visit before returning to Rome. Yes, said the Cardinal, Brother Zeno has become a legend here.

When Brother Zeno and the pope had their reunion, in February 1980, Japanese newspapers gave Zeno's age in guesses varying from eighty-one to eighty-seven, and when he died a year later the estimate jumped to ninety. Whenever asked how old he was he would say, "I, age, don't know." That was because he had been born in Poland during hectic times; few records survive the invasions of Austrian, German and Russian armies.

Zeno and Cardinal Karol Wojtyla first met in Rome in 1971, and by the time Karol became known as John Paul his fellow Pole was feeling the weight of accumulated years. The pope, however, found the Zeno of Japan still humorous, charming and gentle. He had long been a familiar figure on the streets with a white, flowing beard, battered hat, worn-out shoes and a much-patched leather satchel.

Zeno Zebrowski, a member of the Order of Friars Minor, was born on a farm in Poland and worked as a farmer, tailor, cobbler, miner, ironworker and soldier before entering the religious order in 1924. He came to Nagasaki, six years later, with Father Maximillian Kolbe to help print the magazine, *Seibo no Kishi*.

He never really learned to manage the Japanese language. Nor the English language.

A book written about him was titled, *Zeno, No Time to Die*! That was something he had said one day when so busy he had no time to think of death. When reporters asked him how he felt about being honored by the government for his social work, he pointed to the medal on his chest and said, "This, no need in heaven." Two of his much-quoted observations are: "Human beings, I say, all same" and "It's the heart, not words" (that really matters).

The government first took notice of Zeno right after the war. Cities were in ruins. Japanese civilians and soldiers, returning from Korea, Manchuria, Taiwan and China, sought shelter in stations and in underground passages and built shacks under railroad bridges. Food and clothing were scarce. Where to turn!

Wherever the eyes of despair looked they saw Brother Zeno dressed in black soutane, with a rosary around his waist. In his familiar black bag, he carried goods collected from various quarters, including those of the U.S. Army, and distributed them to the needy.

At the time of floods, earthquakes or other catastrophies, he had the ability to put new life into those who had lost hope. He showed them how to help themselves. He restored self-respect.

Zeno became involved in a village in Tokyo called Ant Town. He asked a young woman to look after the orphans there. She became known as Ant Town Mary and is still revered by the Japanese as a holy person long after her death.

The day Brother Zeno died the story of his life was on radio and television and in newspapers all over Japan. His photograph appeared in many places. Soon magazines and books told of his good life.

He may have felt uneasy at the splendid funeral in the Franciscan church in Tokyo. Countless non-Christian Japanese asked to be allowed to hold a general funeral service in a public building in Tokyo to say good-bye to the man with the remarkable eyes.

A schoolgirl read a poem:

> We do not know God.
> But the gentleness of the eyes
> of him who knows God
> Sinks deep into
> our hearts

Brother Zeno had a great impact on the Japanese, even the most sophisticated—as did Father Kolbe, Mother Teresa of Calcutta and Pope John Paul.

When the pope's visit was being planned the cardinal and the missionaries in Japan felt uneasy about it, misjudging how far the country had moved since the days of persecutions. They asked each other: Is this the proper time? Aren't there too few Christians in Japan to rate a visit? Will the Japanese ignore him? Is late winter the best season? Will the media give anything but a minimum of coverage?

Everyone was wrong on every fear. In the worst of weather enthusiastic crowds gathered. The media were more than generous. A vast audience followed, hour after hour, the four-day visit on live television. When the emperor was asked what was the most important thing to happen to him in 1981, he said, "Meeting the pope."

The people were especially touched that John Paul had gone to the trouble to learn Japanese. He did it by having a Japanese priest share breakfast with him every morning for ten weeks. Although he spoke from a prepared manuscript, his accent was more than acceptable.

I asked the cardinal about the "old Christians," the descendants of those who had kept the faith through nearly 300 years of persecutions. The cardinal estimated that there are about 100,000 of them in the archdiocese of Nagasaki, but half refuse to accept the authority of the Roman Catholic Church. They are known as *hanare*, the separate ones. Their faith derives from the time of Saint Francis Xavier.

When persecutions began late in the sixteenth century, Christians went underground. Just before the missionaries were expelled they divided their flocks into cells. Over each they placed four elders, *ojiisan*, and a water man, *mizu-kata*, whose duty it was to baptize children.

When missionaries were allowed to return, in the middle of the last century, many underground Christians refused to accept the French priests. They were accustomed to doing things their own way.

One of their saddest practices today is that of the *chago*. *Cha* means tea and *go* means assembly. Each month the *hanare* meet with the ostensible purpose of drinking tea, but really to offer prayers in common. The prayers suffered in translation while being handed down from generation to generation, so that now they are unintelligible. If a stranger enters while a *chago* is in progress, prayers are suspended and the *hanare* resume drinking tea and chatting. Such suspicion is a relic of the days of persecutions when a stranger might be a member of the secret police.

Such fears were first planted in 1597 when a Spanish sea captain, rescued off the coast of Shikoku, boasted that Christian missionaries were being used to soften up Japan for an invasion by Western powers. When the *shogun* of Kyoto heard this he had seven missionaries and seventeen of their flock arrested. The next day each had the lobe of one ear severed, the mark of a criminal. After being paraded through the streets of Kyoto they were taken to Osaka as a warning to other Christians.

When condemned to be crucified, guards marched them to Nagasaki, a Catholic stronghold. In a hard Japanese winter the 500 miles took the captives twenty-six days. During the trip two more Catholics were taken into custody for helping the prisoners.

On a hill called Tateyama the soldiers tied them to crosses and clamped an iron band around each throat. A sign beneath them read: "Condemned to death on a cross because they preached the forbidden Christian law."

Pope Pius IX canonized the twenty-six martyrs in 1862. A monument to them, fifty-one feet long and eighteen high, stands on the spot where they

died. The artist, Angelico Y. Funakoshi, gave the twenty-six bronze statues each a personality of its own and grouped them to form a singing
choir.

The names are known of some 650 Japanese Christians and their missionaries who were put to death on this hill.

The persecutions began attracting attention outside of the country in
1640 when soldiers killed four Portuguese ambassadors for refusing to
repudiate the faith. The Portuguese government received a warning:
"While the sun warms the earth let no Christians be so bold as to venture
into Japan. Let this be known to all men. Though it were the King of Spain
in person, or the God of the Christians, or the Great Buddha himself, who-
soever shall disobey this prohibition will pay for it with his head."

Behind the monument to the twenty-six martyrs, a little way up the hill,
is a museum dedicated to telling the story of Christianity in Japan, beginning with August 15, 1549, the day that Saint Francis Xavier landed not
far from Nagasaki. When Francis left two years later there were only a few
hundred converts in Japan, but when Christianity was outlawed thirty-five
years later the Catholic community had grown to 200,000.

This rapid growth frightened the rulers. To stop it they devised punish-
ments that were horrendous. Burning at the stake and beheading were considered too humane, and so every conceivable form of torture was tried.
For instance, a sketch in the museum shows a man kneeling on a sharp
piece of wood while being interrogated. One by one logs were stacked
onto his shoulders.

An Englishman, Richard Cocks, described in 1619 how he saw "fifty-
five persons of all ages and both sexes burnt alive on the dry bed of the
Kamo River in Kyoto. Among them were little children of five or six years
old in their mothers' arms, crying out, 'Jesus receive their souls.'"

A favorite form of execution was to hang the victim upside down over a
pit of excrement. To give the blood some vent, and to keep the victim alive
longer, a slight incision was made behind each ear. Some of the stronger
ones survived more than a week in this position, but the majority did not
survive more than a day or two. A Dutch resident in Japan told of a young
woman enduring this for fourteen days before she died. He said, "Some of
those who had hung for two or three days assured me that the pains they
endured were wholly insufferable, no fire nor any other torture equalled
their long drawn-out violence."

The museum displays metal plaques bearing faint images of Christ crucified, images worn smooth by thousands of feet trampling them to assure
authorities of a disdain for the Christian faith. When Christians trampled

on the image of Christ they sometimes went home and scourged themselves with whips now on display in the museum.

Not many years ago a farmer near Nagasaki gave a Catholic priest an antique sign that had been posted in his village 300 years ago. No one can read it, said the farmer, because the characters are archaic. The priest took the sign to Tokyo and asked a scholar to make a translation. It turned out to be the law demanding the persecution of Christians.

It listed several rewards: For information against a priest, 500 pieces of silver; for information against catechists, 300 pieces of silver; for information against those who retract their apostasy, 300 pieces of silver; for information against those who shelter Christians, 100 pieces of silver.

The sign refers to a "group of five," a spy system used during the years of persecution. The whole nation was divided into groups of five persons. Each member of the group was held responsible for the other four. If a Christian were found in any group and had not been informed on by a member of his group, the other four members were punished with him.

Of the many stories recorded in the museum in Nagasaki one of the most interesting is that of the Simabara uprising. The strange thing about the uprising is that Christians in the districts of Amakusa and Simabara accepted persecution for years and did not join non-Christians in an uprising until taxes became excessive.

Even in times of poor crops and famine the lords of Amakusa and Shimabara were inventing new taxes. They even established birth and death taxes and taxes of hearth, door and window.

Failure to pay meant torture and even death. Many were wrapped in coats of rice-straw called *mino* and set afire. The contortions of the flaming victims came to be called the *mino* dance.

When the daughter of a village headman was publicly burned for failing to pay a tax, her father and several villagers killed the tax collector. At the same time a group of *samurai*, out of work because they were Christians, decided to revolt against their rulers. They chose a sixteen-year-old boy, known as Amakusa Shiro, and called him "a leader sent from heaven," feeling that this would unify the people and put some spirit into them.

It worked well enough to capture Hara Castle in Shimabara in October of 1637. An army of 100,000 soldiers, led by the *shogun's* best generals, failed to retake the castle and suffered heavy losses.

After two months the Dutch, in the interest of better trade, decided to curry favor with the *shogun* by sending a warship from their trading post in Hirado. For fifteen days they shelled the castle from out at sea, beyond the range of resurgents' guns.

The rebels surrendered when food and ammunition were gone. Amakusa Shiro and 37,000 of his followers were slaughtered. Among them were 14,000 women and children.

Takegoshu, a Japanese historian, estimates that 250,000 Christians were martyred or exiled during the 250 years of persecution.

A desire for world trade eventually caused the Japanese government to ease up on the persecutions. But Christianity was still unwelcome even though missionaries were allowed to return.

From the French windows of Cardinal Satowaki's study we looked at the charming Gothic church, only a few yards away, the spot where Catholicism in Japan was reborn. When the church was dedicated, February 19, 1865, not one Japanese attended the ceremony; the police had warned against it. The pastor, Father Petitjean, could not even speak to anyone without fear of getting that person into trouble, and so he kept to himself and the church remained locked.

On March 17, a month after the lonely dedication, the priest looked out of the window of his house and saw a dozen people, men, women and children standing before the locked door. He was struck by their respectful demeanor which indicated that they were attracted there by more than curiosity.

When he opened the church door the Japanese followed inside. He approached the altar and knelt to pray. A middle-aged woman knelt beside him and asked, "Where is the altar of Mary?" and "Do you follow the pope in Rome?" Satisfied with the answers the Japanese said, "all of us have the same heart as you." The questions had been handed down from generation to generation, for tradition said that these would help separate the real from the fraudulent.

Soon so many Japanese began coming to Oura church that Father Petitjean was alarmed, fearing the police might interfere. So, he and his parishioners met very early or very late, or on days of bad weather, or at any time that the police might not be on the alert.

Many more hidden Christians were discovered. A man who had come from the Goto Islands to see a doctor told the French pastor at Oura church that his ancestors had fled to the islands 200 years earlier to escape persecution and that at least a thousand Christians were still living there.

On the other side of town, in the Nagasaki section know as Urakami, about 1,300 Christians contacted priests and an equal number were discovered in the neighboring mountains. Four temporary "chapels" were started in the Urakami section where priests went at night, for police continued issuing secret orders that no Japanese should visit a priest.

A bloodless persecution broke out. The cathedral of Urakami now stands on the spot the courthouse and prison stood when Catholics were tried and imprisoned before being sent into exile. This new cathedral, with its 8,883 parishioners, is the largest parish in Japan. The old one, known as the largest church in the Far East, stood a hundred yards from Ground Zero. (Since Nagasaki was the Christian center of Japan a high percent of the 73,884 people killed and the 74,909 injured were Catholics when the bomb fell that morning in August of 1945.)

All persecutions ended because of pressure brought by foreign governments. When Prince Iwakura's delegates traveled through Europe and the United States, "seeking knowledge throughout the world," they were constantly asked, "Why does Japan persecute Christians?" Two of the ministers finally persuaded their government that it could not get terms for a treaty so long as the old edict lasted. That did it. Notice-boards forbidding Christianity came down in 1889. Persecution ceased, not for any spiritual reason, but for the sake of better trade.

I spoke of what a long way Japan has come since the days of persecutions. Yes, the cardinal said, he is aware of the great changes even within his lifetime. And although optimistic, he tried to make me realize how long it takes to develop a mature Christian culture.

As an example of what he meant he told of his own village, not far from Nagasaki; from a population of less than 2,000 it has given the Church more than a 100 nuns, 30 priest and 2 cardinals, the other being the late Cardinal Taguchi, of Osaka. Of the 72,000 Catholics in the archdiocese of Nagasaki, and the 450,000 in Japan, only a small percentage have such a deep tradition of Christianity behind them.

"There must be a traditional concern for the spiritual life," he said. "One that does not tolerate poor values. It is a depth that forms only after several generations of Christianity. In many parts of Japan, priests and sisters and bishops have an intellectual faith, but not enough of it in their hearts. They became Catholics as adults, and so the deep grain is not there."

As Father Flinn and I started down the stairs, the cardinal's parting admonition was: "Write only for the honor and glory of God. Don't write to make the devil happy."

With this background information about the history of Christianity in Japan, Father Flinn and I began a tour of the islands by bus, boat and train. We visited many of the seventy-one Columbans. A few are chaplains and teachers, but the greatest number are assigned to thirty-nine parishes.

One parish is in Tokyo. The rest are scattered through Chiba and Kanagawa prefectures near Tokyo; through Wakayama prefecture, in the southern part of the islands of Honshu, and through Fukuoka, Kumamoto and Oita prefectures on the southern island of Kyushu.

Wherever we went I was impressed with the good feeling between the missionaries and the people. When the first Columbans arrived, in the fall of 1935, they admired their parishioners as educated and cultured, but the closeness was never really there. Everything connected with the Church was scrutinized as "a foreign influence" by a powerful group in Japan opposed to Christianity. Conscious of the opposition, Japanese Catholics were not anxious to antagonize authorities. They still remembered the old persecutions.

By the time the war began the Columbans were in Korea. When they returned, shortly after the war, they were appalled by the sight. Standing in the ruins, watching "people coming up out of the ground like gophers," they marveled at humanity's will to live.

In moving about Japan, I often thought that if I were a missionary I would prefer to be stationed here. The Columban Fathers are also in Korea, Taiwan, Pakistan, China, Peru, Fiji and the Philippines. Why Japan is the country that best suits me I will try to explain.

·26·

An Admirable People

As Father Flinn and I traveled through Japan, I kept being surprised by my reactions. This had begun on the ten-hour flight from San Francisco to Tokyo, while sitting next to a Japanese man of about my own age. To use an old-fashioned expression, he seemed "a gentleman of breeding." In the war he probably fought for the emperor on the other side. Maybe he, too, was in Burma in 1944. What if we had met in the Kachin hills?

Forty years ago neither of us could have guessed the dominant reaction I would get from this trip: My recurring feeling, from beginning to end, was that the Japanese are an admirable people.

In the troubled year of 1945 their cities were rubble. Fire bombs were most effective on old houses with frames of wood, thatched roofs and bamboo walls. A hundred thousand people suffocated on the night of March 9 in a firestorm. War destroyed a million homes in Japan that spring and killed nearly 2 million people. The climax came in August at Hiroshima and Nagasaki.

In Nagasaki I stood at Ground Zero, nearly forty years later, and copied the statistics: 18,409 houses destroyed, 73,884 people killed, 74,909 injured. It was awesome standing at the black pillar comparing what meets the eye today with this same scene of 1945. Old photographs show pieces of rubble, almost of uniform size, stretching away to the mountains; now across the same expanse extends a lovely city.

A proud nation was occupied by a foreign power for the first time in history. Yet the Japanese seemed endowed with hard realism: We have lost the war, and that's that.

The phoenix really can be reborn from the ashes. The Japanese proved it by turning defeat into a victory of sorts. Best of all, they did not use disaster as an excuse to feel sorry for themselves. That is what I most admire.

An Australian nun, who had spent more than twenty years among the Japanese, said at the end of the war: "Now as never before they are showing what character and reserves of strength they possess. But they are suffering behind smiling faces."

An Englishman said: "I have seen them at the height of their power and I came to dislike them intensely. Returning to Japan I now see them in defeat and, you know, they are a great people."

The personal discipline of the Japanese is what struck me most favorably. I found it in every part of the country.

Courtesy, a mark of discipline, shows in the quality of service. Taxi drivers, waiters and shop girls seemed pleased that I was there. Such civility is not offered in expectation of a better tip, for tipping is not done in Japan. Not knowing that, I made the mistake of leaving a tip in a coffee shop. The waitress pursued me two blocks down the street to return it. What she said I could not understand, but someone explained that she was telling me that no one should be tipped for performing a kindness, and that it is disagreeable to be reminded that one does things for others for the sake of money.

Such civility so delighted Isamu Noguchi, an American sculptor, that he visited Japan often. He found that even in humble pursuits there is caring. "It would seem to me," he said, "a maid servant in a Japanese inn and a Japanese farmer do their work more willingly because they take pride in what they are doing, not just because they are paid to do the work."

Personal discipline is also indicated by Japan's literacy. About ninety-eight percent of the population can read. Japan seems to take education more seriously than any other country in the world.

The belief that knowledge is more important than money begins in the home. This brings to mind the immigrant parents in the United States who used to drum into the heads of their children, "Get a good education! Nobody can take that from you. Money you can lose, but a good education stays with you." Those immigrant parents, often illiterate themselves, reared children who became distinguished professionals and made the United States a leader of the world. This attitude, I believe, helps the Japanese get ahead even more than does advanced technology.

Their concern for education shows in many ways. For example, the driver on a bus might turn the radio to something educational, say a lecture on children's health care, rather than to rock music. Educational television thrives. Language courses and courses directed at special groups enjoy large audiences.

A man on a job is expected to keep learning. Housewives are taught to do their work better. Adult-education courses are filled. The 4 million Japanese who travel abroad each year see the trip as a chance to learn new things. The number of new books published annually in Japan, 32,000, is about the same as in the United States; newspaper circulation, 67 million, is the same as in the States where the population is nearly twice as large.

A low crime rate is another reflection of personal discipline. Of course it is no longer so low as when Lafcadio Hearn wrote about Japan early in this century, telling of having lived in districts where people left their doors open all night and no case of theft had occurred for hundreds of years.

The crime rate is low when compared with that of Western countries. In 1980 there were 1.4 murders per 100,000 people as against 10.2 in the United States. The incidence of robbery is 1.9 compared with 234.5 in the States.

One thing that discourages crime is that an offender is apt to be caught. The police are effective largely because the community is behind them. Citizens show a readiness to call them, and the speed of response is remarkable.

The morale of police is high because they know that when they capture a criminal they have not done so in vain. The offender will be punished under the law. Maybe that is because Japan has only 1 lawyer for every 10,000 citizens while the United States has 1 for every 400.

Civility shows in many ways: Almost everyone looks clean and well-pressed. Litter is rare; so are graffiti. Rarely do you see a car with a crumpled fender, rust spots or in need of washing. I used buses, boats, trains and subways and found none a minute off schedule.

The Japanese have developed the discipline to make things of quality. Those of us over fifty remember when they had the reputation for junky products. No one wanted to give a gift with "Made in Japan" stamped on it; knowing this, one town in Japan, in the 1930s, changed its name to Usa and stamped "Made in USA" on all its products.

Now the Japanese produce things of such quality that they are causing world-wide turmoil. They beat the Swiss at watches, the Germans at cameras and beer, and the United States at radios and automobiles.

I don't mean to give the impression that Japan is Utopia, a state of expanding perfection. Cracks are already showing. The country is beginning to suffer the failure of success, called "advanced nation's disease."

A serious symptom is that young people, reared in affluence, are starting to take for granted the things that their parents knew they had to work for.

Japan's educational system shows signs of decline. It traditionally rested on the notion of *dotoku*, promoting the values of filial piety, loyalty and regard for others. Call it respect and courtesy. *Dotoku* is fading, judging from a white paper issued by the prime minister's office that says of today's youth: "They are devoid of perseverance, are dependent on others, and are self-centered."

Students threaten their teachers, even pull knives on them. High-school principals show a loss of nerve by fighting among themselves as how to handle delinquents. At graduation in 1983, police guarded more than ten percent of the junior high schools.

Old people are also causing problems, but in a different way. Since Japan is getting very old very fast, there is danger that the pension fund will become insolvent. The elderly of Japan still have a better life than those in most of the world, but the tradition of living out one's life in the bosom of the family is a thing of the past. Much of the story can be told in one statistic: A tiny Tokyo apartment costs at least $83,000, and most are much more.

The demands made by materialism may be getting too abrasive, observed a Columban, the pastor at Odawara, near Mount Fuji. He told Father Flinn and me of a rebel he had met lately:

"A man near here works in a bank. He is well up toward the top. The other night he came here to the rectory at ten o'clock. He was on his way home, but stopped here first because he did not want to take his troubles to his wife. He said that he rarely gets home before eleven at night. He even works on Saturday and brings home a stack of work, and is often at it until dawn. He sees his children only when they are asleep. 'I am fed up to the teeth,' he told me. 'But what can I do! I have a family to support.' It is evident that he is at the end of his tether.

"The people came through a period of having nothing," said the Columban. "They worked like slaves to get back on their feet. It was a heady experience and they were happy in their materialistic prosperity. A dozen years ago the first signs of disillusionment began to show. People are beginning to realize that there is more to life than material prosperity."

Resentment from without is another threat the Japanese face. As the defeated enemy they enjoyed a certain sympathy, but after creating the second most powerful economy they found themselves on the receiving end of anger from all over the world. (In West Virginia a charity raised money by selling sledgehammer blows on a Toyota.)

The irony is that the United States created this great competitor. The Korean and Vietnam wars brought Japan back into the mainstream.

When, in 1950, Americans became involved in combat once more in Asia, they did not have to depend completely on the manufacture and the repair of weapons in the United States, what with the diligent people of Japan less than an hour's plane trip from Korea. Factories, silent since the war, came into action over night. At the urging of the United States, Japan began to thrive.

Suddenly, she became a major power in the markets of the world. Standards of living soared. Her people lifted themselves up and found a national purpose. Her conqueror had become her ally.

This is remembered as the "Korean boom." It was followed by the "Vietnam boom."

The Japanese feel they are now being used as scapegoats. They are getting blamed, they say, for America's sloppy business practices and for its inefficient labor.

Akio Morita, the co-founder of Sony, a corporation that does 3 billion dollars in sales each year, said: "You have such a spirit in your heart, but now you have forgotten it. Americans have power and courage. America was strong just a few years ago."

The Japanese are also developing a spiritual flaw called nationalism. They keep repeating that Japan is Number One in everything. Such arrogance leads to *hubris*, the pride that precedes the fall.

Thinking people in Japan fear that their country will fall behind because their scientists will not keep pace in research. Unless scientists make basic breakthroughs, manufacturers will always be limited to trivial embellishments.

Up until now Japan has shown more interest in engineers than in research scientists. A technical improvement enjoys an immediate payoff; a basic discovery may take years to bring in dividends.

Some Japanese intellectuals believe that Japan is incapable of keeping up with the rest of the world in basic research. They say that religion, language and education conspire against scientific breakthroughs.

The argument goes that the Judeo-Christian ethic makes clear-cut distinctions between good and evil, while Buddhism teaches that everything in the world is interconnected. So the Western mind is prepared from birth for the confrontational arguments and explicit statements of good scientific debate, while the Buddhist prefer ideas with fuzzy edges.

One scholar described the language as "a tongue full of allusion, suggestion, mood and association of endless poetic nuance and possibility, which is the despair of abstract thinkers and the logical positivists of our world."

The stress on rote learning in the schools, some say, retards creative thinking. They point out that Kyoto University produces more creative alumni than Tokyo University because it encourages more openness of thought. Of Japan's four Nobel prizewinners, three are from Kyoto and one from Tokyo. From Tokyo come political leaders and captains of industry.

Despite any disadvantages the Japanese are determined to make breakthroughs. Their Science and Technology Agency recently published some long-range plans:

They will conquer cancer by 2001.

Their homes will have three-dimensional television by 1997.

Animals and plants will be bred through cell-nuclei fusion by 1998.

There will be a month's advance notice on big earthquakes by 2006.

Hydrogen-powered cars will run on the highways and solar plants will operate in space by 2008.

There will be a practical method for managing low-level radioactive waste by 1994 and of handling high-level waste by 1995.

Science and engineering labs will be built in space in 1995.

While inspiration to accomplish such things cannot be willed, if one works hard enough it might come. Really caring, really wanting, are powerful subterranean forces that gather and grow and finally explode into inspiration. There is value in great expectations.

The Japanese are Oriental enough to know that the future is emergent and cannot be fully planned. The real future always turns out different from the predicted futures. Forty years ago nobody foresaw the Japan of today.

Certainly, I did not foresee my personal reactions. As Father Flinn and I traveled about I often looked at Japanese my own age and was pleased not to feel resentment. They might just as well have been Greek, Spanish or Filipino. Only once did I feel a twinge; it was in Kyoto on Constitution Day. when the streets were lined with large white flags featuring a great red sun. A symbol caused a twinge that flesh and blood could not.

I told a Columban in Fujisawa about my attitude toward Japanese war veterans and he said: "They feel the same about you, but their parents do not. Those in their eighties still hold hatred in their hearts, and sometimes make it a matter of confession."

Forty years ago we were supposed to disapprove of the Japanese, Italians and Germans. And approve of the Chinese and Russians. In a short time those attitudes became upended. Change is so persistent that each morning you need to get up long before reveille to find out what is the uniform for the day.

·27·

Deaths by Violence

When the Columban seminary in County Galway was dedicated, on a June afternoon in 1918, Thomas O'Dea, the bishop of Galway, said, "You won't be any good at all, you know, until some of you are knocked on the head out there in China. You will want a martyr's room here in Dalgan."

No such room was added, nor was it included in the plans when the new seminary was built, thirty years later, at Navan, in County Meath. Had a martyr's room been added it would have begun displaying plaques eleven years after Bishop O'Dea made the prediction.

The first Columban to die by violence was Father Timothy Leonard. At dawn on July 15, 1929, bandits of the Red Army captured him while he was saying Mass. As the assailants rushed the altar the priest reached for the ciborium. A bandit struck his arm with a rifle butt, scattering the consecrated particles. Other bandits trampled on them.

After ripping the priest's vestments from him, the fanatics bound him with ropes. They also bound the Mass server. Upon their demand for money, Father Leonard said that he would give them all he had, about $100, if they would release the boy, which they did.

While the priest knelt in prayer the Reds smashed tabernacles, broke vases and shredded vestments. They jeered at him and jerked on his ropes with such vehemence that he fell forward to the floor striking his face, receiving the first of many wounds.

The Reds marched Father Leonard up to the mountains, twenty miles from the church, and there he and a dozen other captives were put on trial. The judges were the commander of the Communist detachment, age twenty-six; his chief of staff, age twenty; and the head of the political bureau, age twenty-nine.

The judges accused the missionary of having broken the law. When he asked what law, the judges said that he practiced religion, and that his Church had "hooked on" with the Kuomintang. The Columban said his Church had nothing to do with politics, but the judges marked his sheet, "condemned."

All captives were held in one room. As each name was called the prisoner was led out to be stabbed to death at the door. Father Leonard's head was nearly severed from his body. An elderly Chinese gentleman, spared because he paid a ransom, told three Catholics the details of what had happened. They put the dead priest in a coffin, on July 20, and carried him to Nanfeng where two Columbans and a Chinese priest said a solemn Requiem Mass. A vast crowd, pagan and Christian, assisted. A Chinese girl at the Mass eventually became a Columban Sister.

A year later the Reds captured Father Cornelius Tierney. When the church bell rang for Mass at dawn, November 13, 1930, two Reds seized the Columban in the town of Shang Tang Hsu. They pinned his arms behind his back and pushed him against the church door, saying, "You are our greatest enemy."

When Father John Kerr, seventeen miles away, heard of this he disguised himself as a coolie and set out with his teacher, Yang Mao, to keep in touch with the captured missionary. The two men put up in the home of a Catholic three miles from where Father Tierney was being held captive, and Yung Mao went into town each day to learn the news.

The news was never good. For instance, Father Tierney had been stripped of his clothes, scourged with bamboo and given a soldier's red coat to wear. His fellow prisoners so admired his spirit that they shared their quilts, tea and rice with him.

A Columban reported to Hanyang: "Pagans especially expressed their indignation openly and fearlessly that such a good man should be made to suffer so. But whatever leniency was extended to others, there was no mercy for a foreigner among these fanatics. They said he came to China as a forerunner of imperialism."

Yang Mao, disguised as a carpenter, entered the Red camp. He found Father Tierney, dressed in the red coat, sitting dazed in a crowd of Red soldiers listening to their leader harangue them. The priest recognized Yang Mao and surreptitiously gave him a letter written in Latin with a Chinese pen saying that the Reds demand $10,000 in ransom, that he has twenty Mass intentions not yet fulfilled, and that he had hidden $500 under a stone near the church door.

For the next three months the Columbans followed the grim story as Father Kerr sent it back bit by bit. To keep in touch with the ever-shifting situation, Father Kerr lived in the mountains, raking leaves with the villagers as a way of keeping his disguise.

At one time Father Tierney was released. The ransom had been paid, the Reds said. This was not true. Perhaps they said this in order to "save face."

Father Tierney had traveled twenty miles when another band of Reds seized him. In groping for something to feel good about the Columbans in Hanyang decided that if he could travel so far he must be well recovered from his severe illness, which they had judged to be malaria.

Father Tierney died at 2:00 P.M. on Saturday, February 28, 1931, and was buried two hours later in a wild mountainous place. This information reached Hanyang in late March, coming from an old pagan woman who had also been held captive by the Reds. She said that a doctor had told her that the cause of death was malaria.

Yang Mao made arrangements with the bandits to recover the body. After much discussion they eventually promised him the remains if he would buy them some fountain pens and some watches.

The dependable Yang hired four men to open the grave. He immediately identified the missionary's features. Since no coffin could be bought in this remote place, the coolies carried the corpse for forty miles atop a board.

On foot and in a pouring rain, two Columbans traveled to attend the funeral in Kien Chang. There on April 1, they buried Father Tierney after a Requiem High Mass.

The Chinese have a saying, "Adversity is needed for virtue." With such an abundance of adversity, virtue must have thrived on the missions in those days.

The first Columban to die in the Second World War was Father Francis Douglas. His first parish in the Philippines, in the town of Pillilo, had a church that was falling apart, a rectory that resembled an abandoned factory, and a population of Aglipayans and neglected Catholics.

Before he could begin to make headway the Japanese invaded the islands. During the occupation he kept to his post for two years. His parishioners said that the Japanese finally arrested him because Filipino guerrillas were sneaking in from the hills to go to confession.

For three days Father Douglas stood tied to a pillar in the rear of the church while being tortured, starved and threatened. His face was bloody, one eye was black and swollen, his arms were severely bruised.

Even his captors were impressed with his calm. A Japanese officer told one of the parishioners, "I admire the man. He knows how to suffer. He's been there three days and nights but shows no sign of impatience."

How or when death came is not certain. One day in 1943 several Japanese soldiers led the priest away and no one has seen or heard of Father Douglas since.

The greatest horror of the war came on February 3, 1945, when shelling began and lasted for most of the month. The Americans had landed on Leyte in October and were now fighting the Japanese for possession of Manila. In the district called Malate, the Columban school, used as a hospital for three years, was caught in the crossfire, and so was the lovely Spanish church. At least 500 parishioners died in the siege. Every priest in the parish was killed.

Father McFadden wrote to his Columban superiors: "On Tuesday, February 13th, Father John Lalor together with a Dr. Antonio Lahorra and several of the workers went into their air-raid shelter for a few hours' rest. They had had a particularly busy time in the operating room and were completely exhausted. Shortly after they entered the shelter, a shell crashed into the building just above their heads and all inside were killed instantly— mercifully, as it happened, since the shelter burned furiously. The zone was then, and still is, a combat zone, and nothing could be done about burying the bodies. I was allowed to go down there on the 18th and discovered his body, which the nurse helped me identify. We buried him in the school yard, with bullets flying all around."

In that school yard the children used to greet the Columbans in a chorus of treble voices: "Gud ap-ter-noon Fadder! God bless you!"

The priests answered slowly and distinctly, for the children spoke Tagalog at home: "Good af-ter-noon, chil-dren. God bless you!"

The deaths of four other Columbans in Malate are still a mystery. Fathers John Heneghan, Patrick Kelly, Peter Fallon and Joseph Monaghan were taken captive early in the siege. The surviving parishioners say that the priests and many of the menfolk of the parish were taken from the church and headed toward Pasay. They were never seen again. The prevailing rumor is that they were tortured, covered with gasoline and burned.

A quarter of a century later, October 19, 1970, another Columban died of violence in the Philippines. Two sullen Moro students, one with a pistol and the other with a carbine, stalked across the school playground to within ten feet of a young priest dressed in a white soutane. The priest, about to climb into a jeep, paused and said, "Let's go into my office and talk about it." Without a word they riddled him and he died instantly.

Despite his thirty-six years Father Martin Dempsey had kept the lean, fresh look of a college boy right up to that Monday morning when, as principal of the school at Balabagan, he attended the flag ceremony. He verbally corrected a fourteen-year-old student for an infringement of the rules. The boy became angry and reported the incident to his seventeen-year-old brother. The two of them confronted the priest, threatening to kill him. They departed and a short time later returned well armed.

The students on the playground said that the mayor's sons killed Father Dempsey. Archbishop Patrick Cronin confronted the mayor, but the mayor denied that his sons were guilty.

The only bright spot that Archbishop Cronin remembers from that dark day was that two priests approached him to offer themselves as replacements in Balabagan. Such a courageous commitment lifted his spirit. He knew the priests realized all too well that they were offering to spend their lives in Moro country. The archbishop appointed a scholarly man with a capacity for loneliness.

During the Korean war the Columbans were victims of violence more than at any other time. Harold Henry, having learned a few tricks during the Second World War, somehow managed to stay free, but some of his colleagues did not.

When the Korean conflict broke out, forty-one Columbans were working in Korea. They were divided between two mission territories—the Prefecture of Kwangju, under the direction of Monsignor Patrick Brennan, and the Prefecture of Chunchon, under the direction of Monsignor Thomas Quinlan.

Since Monsignor Quinlan's headquarters at Chunchon was only twelve miles from the thirty-eighth parallel, he heard gunfire within two hours after the North Koreans crossed the border at four o'clock Sunday morning, June 25, 1950. Townspeople of Chunchon began to flee by train and truck to Seoul.

Father Anthony Collier, whose parish was across town, visited Monsignor Quinlan late that evening to say that a few Koreans near his church had been wounded by stray bullets and that he had given them first-aid treatment. His church overlooked a bridge that the Red army would have to cross to enter the city. The monsignor, feeling that there would be severe fighting around the bridge, invited the young priest to stay with him for the time being. Father Collier said he felt he ought to return to his church because if the Reds captured the city he might be of some help to his people.

Two days later Father Collier and his house boy, Gabriel Kim, were seized by Communist soldiers as they walked toward the post office. The two were bound together with ropes and marched toward the river. On the way, without warning, one of the soldiers opened fire with a sub-machine gun. In falling, Father Collier pulled Gabriel to the ground with him.

The soldiers left the two for dead. Gabriel had wounds in the shoulder and throat and lay beside the body of Father Collier a day and two nights, working feebly to free his tied hands from those of the dead priest. When at last he succeeded, he made his painful way to Pusan.

A few days later two other Columbans in the vicinity were executed. Father James Maginn, pastor at Sam Chok, and Father Patrick Reilly, pastor at Mukho. Both could have escaped but preferred to remain with their parishioners, mostly new Catholics who were afraid of the Communists.

On the fourth of July, the soldiers took Father Maginn as he was praying in his little one-room church. They beat him and then, three days later, they shot him to death on a hill just outside of town. They then put pressure on his parishioners to declare themselves Communists, but none went over to them.

Father Reilly played hide-and-seek in the hills for a month and could have continued evading the soldiers had not a Korean, to curry favor with the Communists, betrayed him. They came at night and shot him on the roadside, leaving his body there. The local people buried it.

Monsignor Quinlan was saying his Sunday Mass when Communist soldiers came for him. After shooting up the church, they marched the monsignor and Father Francis Canavan to the first of several prisons. Later they were joined by another Columban, Father Philip Crosbie.

From Chunchon the priests were moved to Seoul, later to Pyongyang, and in October were transferred to an internment camp at Manpo in the far north of Korea. On the evening of October 31, 1950, all the prisoners in the camp were told to pack their blankets and get ready to march on what became known as "the Death March."

Ninety-eight of them died on it, some from exhaustion and some from bullets when they could drag themselves no farther. The march of 100 miles lasted ten days. Father Canavan contracted pneumonia in that part of Korea, which is especially cold and has snows especially deep. He seemed to be recovering but then died suddenly on December 6.

Monsignor Quinlan was released April 9, 1953. When Father Crosbie was released some months later he wrote a book about his three years of imprisonment.

During the war in the southern part of Korea the story was much the same—Columbans had a chance to escape but refused. In Mokpo, Father Harold Henry made arrangements to have the priests on a ship sailing for Pusan. He hurried up the hill to the building, in which he had been captured on the night of Pearl Harbor, and urged Monsignor Brennan to leave. No, he said, it was his duty to stay. Fathers Thomas Cusack and John O'Brien said that they would also stay.

The Communists reached Mokpo early in the morning of July 24. The three Columbans were taken on the fifty-six mile ride from Mokpo to Kwangju by motorcycle. The monsignor and Father O'Brien rode as best they could in the sidecar and Father Cusack rode the handlebars.

The priests were held for several weeks in a Kwangju prison. Then they were marched north to Taejon where they arrived in poor physical condition.

The last news of the three Columbans came from the wife of a Korean judge who saw them confined at the Franciscan Monastery in Taejon. She said that when the Red troops prepared to hurry north, so as not to be cut off by advancing United Nations troops, there was a massacre at the monastery.

Later neither Father George Carroll, M.M., nor Father Beaudevin, M.E.P., could recognize any of the Columbans among more than a thousand corpses piled up in the monastery garden. The bodies were so decomposed and swollen that the two priests had difficulty recognizing Father Pollet, a man they had known by sight. A well in the monastery garden was filled with bodies that neither priest had had a chance to inspect.

So in the archives of the Society of St. Columban, Monsignor Brennan and Fathers O'Brien and Cusack are recorded as having died in the massacre of Taejon on September 24, 1950.

Twenty-five years later Archbishop Harold Henry told me that during the war in Korea the Columbans lost seven priests, several seminarians, at least 2,000 parishioners, and half of their buildings. All in all, the Communists had put to death 5 bishops, 82 priests and 150 religious and seminarians.

In Burma, on Columban's Day in 1963, Sisters Andrew and Ita were returning to Manbang from Myitkyina, with Father John Walsh at the wheel of the jeep, when they ran into an ambush. The three of them crouched for hours at the edge of the road with bullets whistling all about.

Although they came through that close call unharmed, Father Walsh would soon die trying to be of help to the Sisters. It happened on Monday of Holy Week, in 1964; he set off on his motorcycle for Mogaung to buy some supplies for the clinic. When he failed to return to his parish at Mogokzup by nightfall, his colleague, Father Robert O'Rourke, began to worry about him and set out for Mogaung to inquire as to his safety.

Four miles from Mogaung, Father O'Rourke came upon a search party standing around Father Walsh's body lying face down in a shallow grave with his rosary beads under his face. There were two bullet wounds in the head and one in the chest. On his right leg there were three gashes, apparently inflicted by a *dah*, a long knife commonly used in Burma. The Kachins and the Burmans blamed the murder on each other. The Columbans had to listen and say nothing while accusations and counteraccusations flew back and forth among the warring groups.

Father Walsh's body was taken to Myitkyina where it was buried in the town cemetery on the morning of Holy Thursday. In recalling the Requiem Mass, Bishop Howe said: "The first relief we got from the awful shock of his death came when we priests spent the evening in Myitkyina recalling some of his many stories. How he unfailingly cheered us with his bubbling good humor and inexhaustible anecdotes! I thought that night that this is the way he would have wanted us to remember him."

The most recent death by violence happened on December 14, 1983, in Lima, Peru. Sister Joan Sawyer was working in Lurigancho Prison when a group of inmates decided to gain liberty at any cost. They plotted to take Sister Joan, three Marist Sisters and several social workers as hostages.

With the hostages in hand the prisoners demanded an ambulance in which to escape. When the ambulance was provided, the escapees took the hostages with them. They were no sooner outside the gate when the police started shooting. The ambulance was riddled with bullets from all sides. The hostages lay under the prisoners who were mowed down on top of them. Of all the hostages only Sister Joan was killed. Four bullets struck her and she died instantly.

While the body of Sister Joan lay in the Catholic Church in Cueva, one of the shantytowns of Lima, crowds of people gathered through the night and filed past the coffin. They were the ones she had ministered to for six years.

Cardinal Landazuri and eighty concelebrants officiated at the funeral Mass. Sister Joan's friends took turns carrying her coffin. That is how they walked the six miles from the church to the cemetery called El Angel.

Nearly seventy years have passed since Bishop O'Dea spoke of the need for a martyr's room. Besides the Columbans who suffered violent deaths since then, some seventy have been imprisoned. While such experience did not kill them outright, it shortened their lives. That is why when I walk through the Columban cemetery in County Meath I find that the dates on the stones tell of the many who died young.

·28·

Goat Paths to God

While searching archives in Ireland and traveling the Far East I came to some understanding of what Saint John of the Cross meant when he wrote: "No two men go more than half way on the same road to God." And by exploring the spiritual lives of others, I learned things about myself.

Right off, I learned that I could never be a missionary. So many unpleasant aspects of the work are beyond my bearing.

In Kwangju, Korea, for instance, I could never bring myself to return each morning to the Beggars' Camp, owned by the city and "administered" by an ex-pugilist with a damaged brain. Each day several Brothers of Saint John of God visit the camp to ease some of the anguish of the unaccepted.

The Brothers led me through a dark, fetid barracks crowded with beds each framing a gaunt tubercular body. Just outside the door, urchins grasped at our hands, hoping for attention, aching to be touched. Madmen with distorted faces made inhuman sounds along the corridor. Slovenly women slouched everywhere.

The Brothers searched for a baby that a retarded girl had given birth to the night before. When they could not find it, they feared it might be in a deep hole out back, one used as a toilet.

All of these disinherited mill around inside the crowded compound, which is something of a barnyard. Each morning garbage trucks, making their rounds, collect prostitutes, idiots, orphans and incurables and drop them into the desolation of Beggars' Camp.

Trying to live with an alien culture is something else I would find uneasy. A young priest in the Philippines was having troubles that way when he went to an old missionary for help.

The young man said: "I don't know what to do. I just don't know what to do!"

The old man raised a hand to stop the flow of troubles and asked, "Father, if you were at home, would you know what to do?"

"Oh, yes!" said the young man.

"There now, that is the answer," said the pastor. "Here you do just the opposite."

Another burden that would be difficult for me to bear is summed up in a Jewish saying: "I have tasted everything and have found nothing so bitter as begging."

My heart went out to the priest who had spent eighteen years in Ireland promoting the missions. When I met him in Fiji he said he had never felt at ease with begging. "As you approach the rectory," he said, "you hear the gravel under your feet and someone coming to the door. You never know what reception you will receive. You have the bishop's letter of introduction in your pocket, but you don't dare to use it. And if things go well and you are asked to stay longer, that is the time to leave. You have made a good impression, so don't spoil it."

I said that I, too, would find begging painful, even though it might be for someone else and for a good cause. He said, "That's because we don't have enough humility, I suppose."

For me the most difficult thing to face would be the lack of beauty in the lives of the poor. Without at least a hint of beauty I am disoriented. A kind of beauty is in their lives, I know, but I am blind to it; saints like Mother Teresa of Calcutta discover it every day. So mine is a limiting attitude, a kind of poverty. Flannery O'Connor included the likes of me when she said: "Everybody, as far as I am concerned, is The Poor."

The Columbans who were murdered are not the first to come to mind when I recall the hardships. Those who loom in memory are the ones who daily face the distorted faces of lepers, feel the grasping hands of the forgotten and smell the stench of hunger on the breath. I remember such small things as the time some of the missionaries could not write home for weeks because the ink was frozen in the bottle.

Since I find prolonged agony more haunting than sudden death, I often recall a French priest in Mandalay, one that Father Kehoe spoke of one evening while we were walking along the Irish Sea in Killiney.

"He always kept in the background," said Father Kehoe. "If someone were introduced to him he would withdraw in haste with hands behind his back. He had contracted leprosy in Pondicherry. The disease was in such an advanced stage that he had lost all feeling in his decaying arms and legs. His only fear was of the marauding, hungry rats. They scurried about when he tried to sleep. They could gnaw on him in the dark and he would not feel it."

Another incident that sticks in my mind happened in China. Father Hugh Sands spent three years without seeing a fellow priest. Eventually, he met a Chinese priest disguised as a vegetable peddler. The Columban went to confession to him while walking in a crowded market place.

I recall the loneliness of a Columban, critically ill in a remote part of China, freezing one minute and burning the next. Finally, the sick man got his Chinese catechist to go for a priest. The nearest one was thirty miles away. The trip, through deep snow and severe cold, would take at least a day each way. During the long wait, the missionary, too sick to keep a fire or prepare food, stared into space, seeking to separate reality from delirium. When at last the visiting priest stood in the door the first thing the sick missionary said was, "I've been lying here thinking: If there is no Heaven, aren't we a bunch of damned fools?"

Many of the missionaries that I met are familiar with such ancient agonies as flood, famine and pestilence, recurring themes in a dramatic tragedy. Although they are intelligent enough and educated enough to get well-paying jobs, most live in a way that might be classified as below the poverty line back home.

No one can say that they have been attracted to their work because it is a "good deal." Yet maybe it is a good deal considering that finding your proper place in the world is a great blessing. The ancient Greeks called it happiness.

The whole idea of vocation became a fascination of mine while writing the six books about the Columbans. There is something transcendent about a vocation whether religious or secular. It is that "call of the hero" which Henri Bergson so insistently emphasized. In discussing vocation, a magazine published by missionaries in Fiji said: "In some special way each person completes the universe."

I learned that when a difficult vocation announces itself there is a tendency to recoil from it, to feel inadequate. But then comes a persistent pressure on the spirit that will not be denied.

An elderly nun told me that as a girl she had tried to evade her vocation. She dreaded the arrival of the *Far East*, magazine published by the Columbans; she even tried hiding it away in a drawer, hoping that out of sight would mean out of mind. Finally, she gave in and became a Columban Sister and served for many years as a nurse in China. There she faced civil war, bandits, Red guerrillas, war lords, Japanese invaders and American bombers but always felt she had made the right choice. I thought of her when I saw that poster in a convent in Japan: "The starting points of human destiny are little things." The mission magazine arriving in County Cork, sixty years ago, was one of the little things that started her toward her destiny.

Vocations remain mysteries even to those who feel most at ease with theirs. A priest in Fiji said: "That last time I went to Ireland, people sometimes asked me why I chose to return to Fiji. It wasn't easy for me to give an answer. All I could say was that I feel compellingly that whatever work I have to do in life is to be done in Fiji, not in Ireland."

Whether religious or layman, anyone living life as a vocation "takes the vows." There must be a loyalty to the work, a faithfulness, a sense of serving under divine commission.

The omnipresence of religion haunted me through all my research. No matter where a missionary's vocation takes him he finds an awareness of the sacred. The necessity for belief is so overwhelming that religion is a central theme in history. It may not be a formal religion, but it is at least something that serves the spirit. Since grasping for the transcendent is basic to the human personality, worship is universal. Missionaries do not bring religion to a place: They introduce a specific religion that gives shape and discipline to an awareness that has been there for time out of mind.

I have arrived at a high regard for all religions. They must have started through the intervention of the Almighty and existed through the ages because God wanted them to. It is unreasonable to suppose that all people, in all places and in all times, have been speaking into the darkness to no avail. To belittle another religion is to pit one's opinion against the experience of the species.

I have even come to respect the myths, taboos and superstitions of primitive peoples. Such primal worship is not unfruitful; it fulfills the need at a certain level. "The person can only receive that which he himself is," said Abraham Maslow, an observation similar to William Blake's "As man is, so he sees."

Fénelon, the eighteenth-century French theologian, felt that you should save yourself through your own particular temperament. As a Welsh proverb has it, "We sing with the voices God gave us."

Some people prefer a religion of high intensity, one that puts tensions in the soul and worships with exuberance. Others need tranquility. The tranquil ones are not apt to urge their way of worship on the intense, but the intense often try to impose themselves on others. To care for so many needs, organized religions are the major roads, but still there are many goat paths to God.

Temperaments vary greatly even within a given religion. Some people turn to theology, some to nature, some to mysticism. Those who prefer one are often impatient with those who prefer another. In Julian Green's diary I found: "A priest who is enamored of mysticism tells of his horror of theology: 'It's nothing but straw! And who said that? Saint Thomas. What do you think of that?'"

Some prefer a structured spiritual life and a worship filled with activity; others, finding solitude at the core of their being, prefer the quiet mind. On a poster in a missionary's room I saw a quote from Pope John Paul II: "Let there be only a great silence before God, for only silence is the true prayer." This reminded me of something a shepherd had said: "I am ashamed to speak of God, the word is too big for my mouth."

I was pleased to learn that Plutarch, traveling late in life to write the lives of others, took an inner journey similar to mine. He saw lesser gods as aspects of the one God and sensed universality in various religions.

The followers in each religion that I researched must come to terms with a faith that falls short. The Known God worshiped is picayune compared with the Unknown God beyond all grasp, for a finite human mind falls terribly short in comprehension. This is something to be accepted along with other forms of suffering. There is consolation, though, in knowing that the various religions, flawed as they are, hold things together. Without them there would be even more chaos.

The tides of all religions rise and fall. Doing research I noticed that in days of distress people more readily admit the primacy of God over that of man. During the Second World War, C. S. Lewis observed: "One unexpected feature of life at present is that it is quite hard to get a seat in church." As Plutarch said, "In adversity Antony was most nearly a virtuous man."

As times brighten, an interest in the transcendent fades and a concern for the graspable takes over.

When the Japanese were spiritually inclined, at the end of the war, a Columban interviewed Sanzo Nosaka, the head of the Communist party in Japan. Nosaka said: "We Communists are materialists. Our goal is to make religion disappear." The irony is that, in time, materialism reached Japan not by way of Marxism by through the abundance brought by democracy and capitalism.

I made the mistake of saying that because there is much materialism in

Japan there must also be much atheism. A missionary in Ryujin brought me up short: "The Japanese concept of God may not be the same as ours, but they do have a concept of a Power that ought to be worshiped. I have never met a Japanese who gave me the faintest impression that he might be an atheist."

The same priest said that the spread of Christianity is not up to the missionary, but to the Spirit and to the Japanese. A missionary is merely an instrument of the Spirit.

"The old-time missionary," he said, "used to think that he was more influential than he really was. It is not 'the excellence of the doctrine' that moves people to the Church. What moves them is the Spirit, and that is a mystery.

"The influence that the missionary has depends on the life that he lives. It is not the words of the preacher but the life that he lives that has the first effect. People must first say, 'We would like to know what makes this man tick.' Then they are ready for the doctrine."

I met a young missionary who was not in Japan to give answers but to give witness. An old man came to his door asking for a place to spend the night and for some food. After both requests were granted the old man asked for warm water to wash his burning feet. He was unable to pull off his boots and so the priest pulled them off for him. Because he wore no socks his feet and legs had been worn raw by the rubber. When the missionary wanted to take him to the hospital the old man refused to go, explaining that he had not long to live.

He said that when a doctor told him he had about two weeks to live, he decided to invest his remaining time finding out if Japan had really lost her soul. He began walking, and now the two weeks were nearly up.

"This is the first time since I started that I have been well treated," he said. "Thanks to people like you who come here to show us how we used to be. Kindness and consideration are gone. Those of you from the outside will have to show us the way back."

Each time that I began researching one of my six books I went back sixty years in the archives and was reminded all over again how militant was the Church of my youth, something I had always felt uneasy about. In those days the Church confronted the triumphalism of science, but now the scientist, too, is more humble; even as he speaks of "an exact science" he admits in his heart "well, just about." It is in the realm of mystery that science and religion can find humility and meet.

The missionary has somewhat lightened his burden of dogmas. Since he no longer represents a militant Church he is free of the us-against-them attitude.

When some Columbans were homeless in China during World War II they were offered hospitality in a Baptist compound. At the time the director of the compound wrote in his journal: "I can just hazard a guess as to what our people at home would say if they ever suspected that there was a Catholic bishop and his priests living in our mission here, and that one of the rooms in this residence has been converted into a Catholic chapel where Mass is celebrated every morning."

This sounds so dated now. As Cardinal Bea said in 1964: "The Counter-Reformation is over." The Second Vatican Council made missionaries aware that the Church should cherish whatever good is in the minds and hearts of diverse peoples, no matter what their religion.

While explaining the new attitude, a priest in Tokyo said: "Christ's admonition was, 'Go ye into the whole world and preach the gospel to every creature.' Not convert, but preach. Make the approach. God in his time will give the increase."

Perhaps the most valuable thing the decade of research did for me was heighten my sense of mystery. Some of the missionaries, who relived their lives during the interviews, found an awareness of mystery rekindled. In putting together the bits and pieces into a pattern they saw how God uses ordinary people to do extraordinary things, adopting natural means to bring about supernatural effects.

If a young missionary should ask me for advice, wanting to hear in a few words what I had learned, I would tell him what an elderly bishop from Chile said in a sermon to some Columban seminarians. His closing words were: "Focus on God. God is above ideology, nations, the priesthood, and the Church. Focus on God."